DISCO

INSIDE ISSUE 11: 1 SAMUEL, DANIEL, LUKE

1 Find a time when you can read the Bible each day

2 Find a place where you can be quiet and think

4 Ask God to help you understand what you read

3 Grab your Bible and a pencil or pen

5 Read today's Discover page and Bible bit

6 Pray about what you have read and learned

We want to...
- Explain the Bible clearly to you
- Help you enjoy your Bible
- Encourage you to turn to Jesus
- Help Christians follow Jesus

Discover stands for...
- Total commitment to God's Word, the Bible
- Total commitment to getting its message over to you

Team Discover
Martin Cole, Nicole Carter, Rachel Jones, Kirsty McAllister, Alison Mitchell, André Parker, Ben Woodcraft
Discover is published by The Good Book Company, Blenheim House, 1 Blenheim Rd, Epsom, Surrey, KT19 9AP, UK.
Tel: 0333 123 0880; Email: discover@thegoodbook.co.uk   UK: thegoodbook.co.uk
North America: thegoodbook.com   Australia: thegoodbook.com.au   NZ: thegoodbook.co.nz

How to use Discover

Here at Discover, we want you at home to get the most out of reading the Bible. It's how God speaks to us today. And He's got loads of top things to say.

We use the New International Version (NIV) of the Bible. You'll find that the NIV and New King James Version are best for doing the puzzles in Discover.

The Bible has 66 different books in it. So if the notes say…

Read 1 Samuel 1 v 1

…turn to the contents page of your Bible and look down the list of books to see what page Genesis begins on. Turn to that page.

"1 Samuel 1 v 1" means you need to go to chapter 1 of 1 Samuel, and then find verse 1 of chapter 1 (the verse numbers are the tiny ones). Then jump in and read it!

Here's some other stuff you might come across…

WEIRD WORDS

Grippyfrit
These boxes explain baffling words or phrases we come across in the Bible.

Think!

This bit usually has a tricky personal question on what you've been reading about.

Action!

Challenges you to put what you've read into action.

Wow!

This section contains a gobsmacking fact that sums up what you've been reading about.

Pray!

Gives you ideas for prayer. Prayer is talking to God. Don't be embarrassed! You can pray in your head if you want to. God still hears you! Even if there isn't a Pray! symbol, it's a good idea to pray about what you've read anyway.

Coming up in Issue 11...

1 Samuel: Search for a king

What do you think makes a good leader — what would you look for in a new teacher or team captain?

In the book of 1 Samuel, God's people, the Israelites, are looking for a leader. But they don't always look for the right thing...

We'll read 1 Samuel in three chunks, which each focus on one of three men.

First, there's Samuel, who started serving God when he was younger than you! Next, there's Saul, who goes out looking for his dad's donkeys and ends up being made king of Israel! He's a tall guy, but he falls short of expectations. Third, there's giant-slayer David. He's got loads to teach us about trusting God.

This book is full of strange and exciting moments. But most importantly, it points us to God's perfect King, Jesus!

Daniel: Walk God's way

Living for God is really tough sometimes — especially when the people around you don't.

Daniel was a man who knew how that felt. He and his friends got taken from their home in Israel to serve the Babylonian king (who didn't worship God). Reading about Daniel will show us how to stand out from the crowd by standing up for God!

You've probably already heard of Daniel and the lion's den, but there's loads more to his story than that. For example, have you heard of Daniel and the ten-horned beast? *No?!* Then get ready to find out!

Luke: Jesus the perfect teacher

We dive into Luke's Gospel to listen in on some awesome teaching from Jesus.

It looks like it's almost the end of the road for Jesus — less than a week before He dies — but He's still got loads to say. There are these religious guys who keep trying to trip Him up with tricky questions. But Jesus ALWAYS out-smarts them with His answers. Plus we'll hear Him tell some amazing stories (a.k.a. parables), and even get a heads-up on what the end of the world will be like! It's gripping stuff!

Ready?
Steady?
Let's read!

Samuel: Given to God

Let's dive into the book of 1 Samuel and meet a family even weirder than yours...

THE STORY SO FAR...

God had been great to His people, the Israelites. He rescued them from Egypt, gave them their own country (Canaan) and defeated their enemies loads of times.

In return, the Israelites kept turning away from God and disobeying Him! In the last issue of *Discover* we read how God gave the people judges to rescue them and lead them.

But read Judges 21 v 25

Despite all that God had done for them, they rejected Him and lived their own way.

Now let's meet a woman who **did** still obey God...

Read 1 Samuel 1 v 1-8

Now fill in the missing names.

E_____

was married to

P_____.

They had several children.

E_____ **was also**

married to H_____,

who couldn't have children.

P_____ **teased**

H_____ **until she**

burst into tears.

Think!

How do you react when things at home seem to be going really badly?

- Try to understand how the others might be feeling?

- Just look after yourself?

- Take it out on a parent (or brother or sister)?

- Pour out everything to God, and ask Him to help you?

Tomorrow we'll find out what Hannah does.

The weird thing is that it was God who stopped Hannah from having children (v6). That seems so unfair, but tomorrow we'll see God's great plan kicking into action!

Pray!

Ask God to help you serve Him in your family situation. Thank God that He's got a perfect plan for you, even when life seems tough.

WEIRD WORDS

Zuphite
Descended from a man called Zuph

Worship
Praise God

Sacrifice
Offer gifts to God

House of the LORD
Place where God was worshipped

2

Pray your heart out

1 Samuel 1 v 9-18

Hannah was really upset because she was unable to have children.

But she knew where to take her troubles...

WEIRD WORDS

Priest
He was God's special servant in the temple

Vow
Promise

Anguish and grief
Worry and great sadness

Downcast
Really sad

Read 1 Samuel 1 v 9-11

Hannah told God exactly what was on her mind. And if God gave her a son, she promised to give the boy to God, so that he'd serve God in a special way (v11).

Tick the boxes that describe Hannah's prayer.

self-important	real

same old words

honest	holding back

meaningless words

from the heart	in tears

Think!

Which of those phrases describe your prayers?

_____

_____

_____

_____

Wow!

We can be totally honest with God. We can tell Him what's on our minds, what's upsetting us. God wants us to pour our hearts out to Him. He cares. He listens.

Read verses 12-16

Eli the priest accused Hannah of being drunk! How embarrassing. He wasn't used to seeing people pray in such an honest and tearful way.

Read verses 17-18

*Telling God about her problems had a real effect on Hannah. Draw Hannah's face **before** and **after** praying.*

BEFORE   **AFTER**

Hannah didn't look so miserable any more! She had told God what was getting her down. She knew she could **trust Him** and wait to see what His answer would be.

God won't always answer our prayers in the way we expect. But we can trust that He'll always do what's best for us.

Action!

When you pray, pour your heart out to God. Leave your troubles with Him — He wants to sort them out.
Why not start right now, by talking honestly to God about how you're feeling?

3

1 Samuel
1 v 19-28

Hannah has tearfully asked God to give her a son.

Let's see how God answered her prayer.

Bye bye baby

Read 1 Samuel 1 v 19-20

What did Hannah call her son?
Go back one letter to find out
(B=A, C=B, D=C etc).

— — — — — —
T B N V F M

What does that mean?

— — — — —
I F B S E

— — — — —
C Z   H P E

God heard Hannah's prayers and gave her a son!

It's easy to make promises to God when life is hard, and then forget them when life gets better!

Hannah must have been over the moon with baby Sam, but would she keep her promise?

Find the promise back in verse 11.

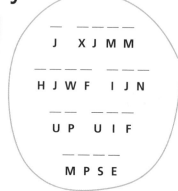

— —   — — — —
J   X J M M

— — — —   — — —
H J W F   I J N

— —   — — —
U P   U I F

— — — —
M P S E

Did Hannah keep her promise?

Read verses 21-28

Weaned
When a baby stops being fed by it's mother's milk (in those days at about 3 years old).

We reckon Samuel was about 3 years old when Hannah left him at the temple. It must have been hard for Hannah to leave the son she had wanted for so long. But she'd promised to give him to God, and knew that God must come first.

Pray!

Do you know anyone with a small baby? Pray that their child will be "given to God" — that he/she will grow up to live for God.

WEIRD WORDS

Sacrifice
Gifts to God (usually animals and crops)

Ephah
About 22 litres

Skin of wine
Wine bottles made from the skin of animals

Raise the praise

**1 Samuel
2 v 1-11**

*God has given
Hannah the son
she asked for. So
she's going to
thank and praise
God loads!*

WEIRD WORDS

Rejoices
Is really happy

**My horn is
lifted high**
God has given me
strength

Deliverance
Rescue

Barren
Unable to have
children

**Humbles
and exalts**
Makes less important
and more important

Prevails
Succeeds

His anointed
God's chosen king

Her prayer is in three parts. *Use the
verses and the word pool to fill in
the gaps.*

children   death   food
guards   heart   holy
knows   life   Lord
poverty   oppose   Rock
shattered   strength
wealth   world

1. Thanking God
Read 1 Samuel 2 v 1-3

My h_____ rejoices in
the L_____. No one is
h_____ like the Lord. No
one is a R_____ like our
God. The Lord is a God who
k_____.

Hannah thanks God for giving her a
son and making her soooo happy!

2. What God is like
Read verses 4-8

God gives s_____
to the weak and f_____
to the hungry. He gives
c_____ to the
childless. He gives people
both d_____ and
l_____.

He gives both
p_____ and
w_____. God is
in control of the whole
w_____!

Hannah praises the Lord because He
is in control of EVERYTHING!

3. What God will do
Read verses 9-11

The Lord g_____
His people. But those who
o_____ Him will be
s_____. God
will give strength to His King.

Hannah praises God for caring for
people who obey Him. But He will
also punish people who reject Him.
Later on in 1 Samuel, we'll read
about how God was with King
David. But the perfect King, who
would come to save God's people,
was JESUS.

Pray!

1. Thank God for specific things
   He has done for you
2. Praise Him for what He's like
3. Praise God for what He will do

5

1 Samuel
2 v 12-17

Little Samuel has begun serving God in Shiloh.

But some of the priests weren't serving God at all...

Pilfering priests!

Priest Puzzler!

Tick (✔) the statements you would expect to be true for God's priests.

Obeyed God's laws ☐

Set a good example ☐

Honest ☐

Put God first ☐

Gentle ☐

God had given the Israelites instructions (they're in Leviticus) about how sacrifices should be offered to God. The priets were allowed to eat some of the meat. God's instructions made it really clear which parts of the meat they were!

Read about one of these rules in 1 Samuel 2 v 12-14

That was the way things should have been done. But Eli's sons were greedily stealing whatever they wanted! They didn't care about God (v12).

Read verses 15-16

*Now put **X**s in the statements that **don't** describe Eli's sons.*

Obeyed God's laws ☐

Set a good example ☐

Honest ☐

Put God first ☐

Gentle ☐

The fat should have been given to God (it was the best part).

But these priests **put themselves before God**. And if anyone stood up to them, they were threatened with violence!

Read verse 17

Eli's sons upset and angered God by disobeying Him.

Pray!

What do you keep doing that offends God?

_____

_____

_____

_____

Will you say sorry to God? Ask Him to help you stop doing these things.

Spot the difference

**1 Samuel
2 v 18-26**

*Spot the
difference
between young
Samuel and Eli's
evil sons...*

WEIRD WORDS

Ministering
Serving

Linen ephod
Priest's clothes

Gracious
Gave her far more
than she asked for

**Mediate/
intercede**
Settle a problem

Rebuke
Telling off

Stature
Size

Read 1 Samuel 2 v 18-21

Notice that little Samuel is serving God (v18). Hannah had asked God for just one son.

And she'd given him to serve God in the temple. But God gave her five more children!

Wow!

God often gives us far more than we ask for. Make sure you notice everything God gives you. And thank Him!

Read verses 22-26

*Spot the difference. Stick an **S** in the boxes that describe **Samuel**, and an **E** in the ones that describe **Eli's sons**.*

> **Didn't serve the Lord (v12)**

> **Refused to listen to their dad (v25)**

> **Served the Lord (v18)**

> **Bad report from the people (v24)**

> **God was pleased (v26)**

> **God was angry (v17)**

Do any of those phrases describe you? (If you say no, you're lying!) Put your own initials in the boxes that describe you.

Are you ever like Eli's sons? You know that you should be pleasing God, but you keep sinning against Him?

Do you try to please God and live for Him, as Samuel did?

PRAY!

Don't hang around! Today would be a great day to say SORRY, and ask God to help you please Him from now on.

Ask God to help you to grow into someone who serves Him with your whole life.

Sons shunned

**1 Samuel
2 v 27-36**

Eli's sons have disobeyed God and angered Him.

Eli told them off, but they ignored him and refused to change. They continued to insult God with their sinful ways.

Read 1 Samuel 2 v 27-29

Fill in the missing vowels (aeiou).

God sent a messenger to Eli. He spoke God's words. He said:

Why d__ y__ __

sc__rn my s__cr__f__c__

__nd __ff__r__ng?

Why d__ y__ __ h__n__ __r

y__ __r s__ns m__r__

th__n m__? (v29)

God had been so kind to Eli's family. He had given them the fantastic privilege of serving God in a special way, as priests. But Eli had let his sons disobey and dishonour God. He had put his sinful sons before God.

Think & pray!

Do you sometimes disobey God, rather than risk offending your friends or family?
(For example going along with rude jokes.) Ask God to help you stand up for Him more.

Read verses 30-34

God punished Eli's whole family. Both of Eli's sons would die, and none of the family would live a long life. Eli's family had sinned against God, so God rightly punished them. But it wasn't all bad news...

Read verses 35-36

I w__ll r__ __s__

__p a f__ __ thf__l

pr__ __st

Despite the sin of Eli's family, God would find a priest who would serve Him faithfully, and lead God's people in worshipping Him.

Wow!

Never forget how seriously God treats sin. And remember, whatever people do, God's plans can't be stopped!

8

1 Samuel
3 v 1-10

Feeling sleepy?

Well, God has a wake-up call for all of us...

Wake up call

Read 1 Samuel 3 v 1

In Old Testament times, God spoke to His people through prophets. These prophets sometimes had visions, telling them what God wanted to say to His people.

The Israelites had stopped listening to God, so He didn't speak to them much any more. But God was so good to His people that He was going to start speaking to them again through SAMUEL.

Read verses 2-7

God was calling out to Samuel, but Samuel hadn't worked out that something amazing was happening!

SAMUEL!

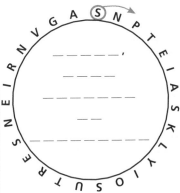

Wow!

These days, God doesn't usually speak to us through prophets, visions or late-night awakenings! We now have God's Word in the Bible. The Bible is God's message to us!

Action!

Every time you read the Bible, make sure you pray first. Ask God to "speak, for your servant is listening".

WEIRD WORDS

Ministered
Served

Word of the Lord
God speaking to His people

Ark of God
Really special wooden box. The 10 Commandments were kept in there.

Read verses 8-10

God was so patient with young Samuel!

*What did Samuel finally say to God (v10)? To find out, write down **every second letter** on the wheel at the top of the page, starting with the **top S**.*

Pray!

Thank God that He speaks to you through His words in the Bible. Ask Him to teach you loads from the Bible and help you put it into practice.

9

**1 Samuel
3 v 11-18**

God has chosen young Samuel to be His prophet — the one who'd speak God's message to the Israelites.

What an amazing honour for a young lad!

WEIRD WORDS

Uttered blasphemies
Said insulting things about God

Restrain
Stop

Swore
Promised

Atoned
Paid for, forgiven

Get the message?

God's first message to Samuel is a hard one to swallow.

Read 1 Samuel 3 v 11-14
Today's missing words can be found in the wordsearch.

S	K	C	U	R	S	E	L	S	Q
A	A	G	Q	C	E	P	B	V	H
F	A	M	I	L	Y	X	M	I	Y
R	C	S	U	R	U	E	P	S	L
A	M	V	B	E	A	G	U	I	N
I	H	P	S	F	L	J	N	O	D
D	I	S	O	B	E	Y	I	N	G
A	L	I	N	C	U	R	S	E	N
R	N	F	S	E	L	I	H	Z	K

The Lord told

S_____ that

He would p_____

Eli's f_____

because Eli didn't stop

his s_____ from

d_____ God.

Read verses 15-17

**Samuel was a_____
to tell E_____ about his
v_____. But Eli
threatened to c_____
Samuel if he didn't tell
Eli everything.**

Wow!
God's Word (the Bible) contains stuff that's hard to tell people. Just think how many people ignore the 10 Commandments. But we should have the courage to tell people the truth from God's Word.

Samuel told Eli the truth. And look at Eli's answer...

Read verse 18
Eli totally accepted God's Word, even though it was really tough on him.

Pray!
Ask God to help you to accept what He says, like Eli did. And ask Him for the courage to tell people what the Bible says.

1 Samuel
3 v 19-21

So Samuel is God's chosen prophet.

God will speak to all of the Israelites through him!

Word perfect

Read 1 Samuel 3 v 19

Now rearrange the backwards words so they make sense.

EHT   HTIW   PU   DROL
LEUMAS   SA   EH   SAW
WERG

THE   LORD   [ ]
[ ]   [ ]
[ ]
[ ]   [ ]

God was with Samuel, helping him to live for God and serve the people. Everything Samuel said was true.

Pray!

Spend time asking God to be with you, helping you to grow into someone who serves God with your whole life.

Read verses 20-21

EHT   HGUORHT
SIH   DROL   DROW
OT   DELAEVER
FLESMIH   LEUMAS

THE   LORD   [ ]
[ ]   [ ]   [ ]
[ ]   [ ]

Wow!

Today God still reveals Himself to us through His Word. We can only get to know God by reading the Bible.

Read the first sentence of 1 Samuel 4 v 1

S'LEUMAS   LLA   EMAC
LEARSI   OT   DROW
[ ]   [ ]
[ ]   [ ]
[ ]

The Israelites had constantly rejected God and sinned against Him. Yet God gave them another chance by speaking to them through Samuel.

Pray!

Thank God that He is so kind and loving to His people. Thank Him that He speaks to us through the Bible.

Raiding the ark

**1 Samuel
4 v 1-11**

The Israelites are fighting their enemies, the Philistines.

*No problem —
God always gives them victory.*

Doesn't he?!

WEIRD WORDS

Deployed
Sent

Covenant
An agreement where God said He'd be with the Israelites and they said they'd obey Him

Cherubim
Angel-like creatures

Hebrews
Israelites

Read 1 Samuel 4 v 1-3

Shocker! The Israelites were defeated. *So what did they decide to do? (v3)*

The ark of the covenant

Large wooden box with the 10 Commandments in it. It was a big reminder that God was with His people. It also reminded them of the great promises He had made. (Sometimes called Covenant Box or Sacred Chest)

If the ark was with them, they were bound to win! Weren't they?

Read verses 4-9

The Israelites were now...

a) totally bored ☐

b) scared stiff ☐

c) over the moon ☐

The Philistines were now...

a) totally bored ☐

b) scared stiff ☐

c) over the moon ☐

So who do you think is going to win the battle?

Read verses 10-11

A disastrous, death-filled defeat for the Israelites. They had trusted in the ark to save them, not God. They used the ark like a lucky charm. They should have asked God to save them!

And now they've let God's enemies capture the ark!

Wow!

**church   crosses
communion   baptism
saying the right things**

These things are important, but none of them make us Christians. We need to turn to Jesus for forgiveness. Only He can change our lives around.

Eli's end

1 Samuel
4 v 12-22

Three disastrous things have happened...

1. **Many Israelites have been killed**

2. **The ark of the covenant has been stolen**

3. **Eli's sons have died**

Back home, Eli was nervously waiting for news of the battle.

What do you think Eli would be most upset about?

a) Israel's defeat ☐

b) death of his sons ☐

c) losing an old box ☐

Read 1 Samuel 4 v 12-18

Okay, so the ark was much more than an old box! It showed that God was with His people. So when they lost the ark, they knew God had left them too. It was such a shock to poor Eli that he fell off his chair and died.

Read verses 19-22

Another desperately sad story.

Cross out all of the Bs, Cs and Js to reveal what the woman said (v21).

T H B B E G C J L O J J R Y H C B

A B S D J C E P A J R T C C E D C

J B F R O B B M I S R J A B E L C

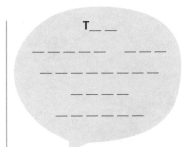

T_ _ _

_ _ _ _ _ _   _ _ _ _

_ _ _ _ _ _ _

_ _ _ _

_ _ _ _ _ _ _

Both Eli and his daughter-in-law died thinking that God had left Israel.

But this wasn't the end of the story...

Chapters 5 to 7 show how the Philistines returned the ark and the Israelites started trusting and obeying God again.

And God had the prophet Samuel leading the people in living for Him!

For the details, read through chapters 5 to 7 yourself! We'll come back to Samuel later in this issue.

Pray!

Read Deuteronomy 31 v 6. Thank God that He has promised never to leave His people (Christians)!

WEIRD WORDS

Benjaminite
From the tribe of Benjamin

Ichabod
Means "no glory"

Glory
The brilliance of having God with them

13

Daniel: Walk God's way

Daniel
1 v 1-7

We're going to fastforward through history to the book of Daniel.

It's brilliant! It's got amazing dreams, fierce lions, fire walking and some really weird stuff going on.

WEIRD WORDS

Babylon
City 100s of miles from Jerusalem

Besieged
Surrounded and attacked

Nobility
Rich and important people

Aptitude
Ability

Literature
Books

But Daniel's book is really about how **God is in control** even when it doesn't seem like it. It's also about how we can live God's wise way even when it seems tough.

Before we dig into Daniel, we need some background info...

DANIEL – HISTORY FILE

- God took His people to the promised land, Canaan. It became known as Israel.

- But the Israelites kept turning away from God.

- After King Solomon died, the kingdom split in two.

- The big northern bit was called Israel. The smaller southern bit was called Judah.

Daniel's story begins in Judah around 605 BC.

Read Daniel 1 v 1-2

... and fill in the missing words.

> King N_____
> of B_____ attacked
> God's special city of
> J_____ in the
> kingdom of J_____.
> The Babylonians stole some
> of the special treasure from
> God's temple. They also
> took some of the best men
> from Judah...

Read verses 3-7

> Top young men from Judah
> were picked to be trained to
> serve the king of Babylon.
> They were taught all about
> Babylonian I_____
> and I_____
> (v4). These men included
> D_____, H_____,
> M_____ and
> A_____. They were
> all given new names (v7).

Things were looking bad for God's people. But who was really in control? Who had given Judah into the Babylonians' hands? (v2)

> The L_____!

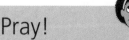

Pray!

God had caused all these things to happen. He was in complete control! Ask God to teach you more about Himself as you read Daniel's story.

Food for thought

**Daniel
1 v 8-16**

Daniel and his three friends have been captured by the Babylonians.

They're being trained to serve King Nebuchadnezzar.

Let's see how it's going...

Read Daniel 1 v 8

We don't know exactly what was wrong with the royal food and wine. But Daniel thought he'd be offending God if he ate it. So he refused to eat it.

Wow!

Sometimes we have to make a stand for God. If we know that something is wrong, then we shouldn't do it, even if it means we'll get teased.

Watching a certain movie, going along with the crowd at school — if it's wrong, refuse to do it.

And if you're not sure if it's right or wrong, make a stand and refuse to do it anyway. Play safe for God.

Action!

What do you need to make a stand about?

_____

_____

_____

_____

Read verses 9-10

God was in control! He made the official sympathetic to Daniel.

God isn't just in control of the big things in life. He's in control of everyday things too! But the official was still too scared to give Daniel different food...

Read verses 11-14

Daniel didn't give up.

Complete his plan by filling in the first letters of words.

Please __est your
__ervants for __en
__ays. Give us __othing
but __egetables to __at
and __ater to __rink. Then
__ompare us with the men
eating the __oyal __ood.

Read verses 15-16

After 10 days eating their own food instead of the king's, they looked better than all the other men! Daniel made a stand for God and God did amazing things!

Pray!

Ask God to help you make a stand for Him, so that you do the things you wrote down under Action! And actually try hard to do them. It will be tough, but worth it.

Testing times

15

Daniel
1 v 17-21

Daniel and his three friends were captured and taken to Babylon.

Bravely, they stood up for their beliefs and refused to eat unclean royal food.

How did God help them?

Read Daniel 1 v 17

... and untangle the anagrams.

God gave them

k_____

w o n d g l e e k

and understanding. And

D_____ could

l a i D e n

understand d_____

r e d s a m

and v_____.

s i v i n s o

God helped them become the best students in Babylon! And He gave Daniel the ability to understand dreams. That would come in handy later on.

Wow!

What are you good at? School? Sport? Acting? Cooking? Cheering people up?

_____

_____

It's God who gives us all our knowledge and abilities. So we should thank Him and give Him the glory.

What do you think of this word?

EXAMS!

_____

Today is exam day for Daniel and his friends. The king himself is questioning them about the stuff they've learned in Babylon.

Time to find out how well they did.

Read verses 18-21

They were _____ times better than the best of the rest!

Why did they do so well? (v17)

```


```

It was all down to God! He was in total control. God had allowed the king of Babylon to capture these men and God gave them the brains to be top of the class. Now they had become King Nebuchadnezzar's servants. God's plans are coming together.

Pray!

Thank God that He's in control of everything. Thank Him for the abilities He's given you. Ask Him to help you use them to serve Him.

16

Horror scope

**Daniel
2 v 1-19**

*King
Nebuchadnezzar
was the most
wealthy and
powerful man
around. But
he still had
nightmares...*

*Your challenge
today is to use
the words down
the centre to
complete this
strange story.*

WEIRD WORDS

Astrologers
Men who looked at
the stars to predict
the future

The gods
Fake gods

Tact
Being careful in what
he said

Mercy
Undeserved kindness

Read Daniel 2 v 1-13

Nebuchadnezzar had bad
d_____ (v1).
So he gathered all the
m_____
and astrologers to
e_____ the dream
to him (v2-3). He also
wanted them to tell
him exactly what he'd
dreamed. If they could do
it they would get a great
r_____ (v6). If they
couldn't, they'd all be
c_____ to pieces (v5).
They said that it was
too d_____
(v11). The king was
f_____ and ordered
the e_____
of all the w_____ men
in B_____ (v12).
This included Daniel and
his f_____ (v13).

None of the magicians or astrologers
knew the king's dreams. They
were all fakers. Even today, some
people claim to tell the future. But
horoscopes and fortune-telling are a
load of rubbish and sometimes evil.
Have nothing to do with them!

(centre words, top to bottom): furious king magicians mercy mystery night pray reward time vision wise friends explain execution difficult dreams Daniel cut Babylon Arioch

Read verses 14-19

A_____ told
D_____ what
the king had ordered
(v15). Daniel went to
the k_____ and asked
for more t_____ so
that he could interpret
the dream (v16). Then
Daniel asked his friends
to p_____ to God
for m_____ and
help (v18). During the
n_____ God revealed
the m_____
to Daniel in a
v_____ (v19).

Wow!
If you find yourself in a tricky
situation... PRAY! Take your
troubles to God and plead
with Him to help you. Get your
friends to pray for you too. God
longs to hear us talk to Him and
He loves to answer our prayers.

Pray!

What's on your mind? What
tough situation do you find it
hard to face? Tell God about it
now and plead with Him for help.

Praise practice

**Daniel
2 v 19-23**

*Daniel and his
friends will be
killed if Daniel
can't tell the king
what he dreamed
about.*

*But God reveals
everything to
Daniel at night.*

Read Daniel 2 v 19-23

God told Daniel the king's dream
and what it meant. Daniel was over
the moon and he praised God for
how great He is.

*Daniel's prayer is full of great truths
about God. Fill in the blanks to
reveal them.*

WHAT GOD HAS

W_ _ _ _ _ and
p_ _ _ _ _ are his (v20).

L_ _ _ _ _ dwells with
    1
    Him (v22).

He knows what's in the
d_ _ _ _ _ _ _ (v22).
    2

God is far more powerful than
anyone. He knows everything.
Nothing is hidden from God.

WHAT GOD DOES

Changes t_ _ _ _ and
        3
s_ _ _ _ _ _ (v21).
    4

Sets up and removes
k_ _ _ _ (v21).
    5

Reveals d_ _ _ and hidden
            6
t_ _ _ _ _ (v22).
    7

God is in control of everything that
happens. He's far more powerful
than kings and presidents.

He also helps us to understand really
difficult things. Through the Bible,
He reveals to us amazing truths
about Himself.

WHAT GOD GIVES

W_ _ _ _ _ (v21).
    8

K_ _ _ _ _ _ _ _
                9

P_ _ _ _ (v23).

Without God we're nothing. He
gives us all our abilities. We have no
reason to boast about what we have
or what we can do.

All good things come from God!

Crack the code.

__ __ __ __ __ __   __ __ __
6 2 4 1 5 9   7 8 3

That's how Daniel reacted when
God answered his prayer. Daniel
thought about his great God and
praise came pouring out of him.

Think & pray!

Read verses 20-23 again.
Do you thank God like that
when He answers your prayers?
Use these verses to praise God
right now.

Glory story

**Daniel
2 v 24-30**

*God showed
Daniel what the
king's dream
was and what it
meant.*

*Now Daniel must
face the king...*

WEIRD WORDS

**Exiles from
Judah**
The young men
the Babylonians
had captured from
Jerusalem

Diviner
Someone who tries
to predict the future

Yesterday we saw how Daniel
praised God for answering his
prayer. But there is another way we
can show our gratitude to God.

Read Daniel 2 v 24-30

*Complete the conversation between
Daniel and King Neb by filling in the
missing **E**s, **I**s & **D**s.*

> Can you t__ll m__ what
> my __r__am was an__ what
> __t m__ans?

> No w__s__ man or
> mag__c__an can __xpla__n
> to you the myst__ry of your
> __r__am. But th__r__ __s
> a Go__ __n h__av__n who
> r__v__als myst__r__ __s.
> (v27-28)

Daniel made sure that the king
knew exactly who was wise enough
to reveal the mystery of his dream.

HE GAVE ALL THE
GLORY TO GOD

Think!

When things go well for you, do
you boast about it or remember
that God was behind it? When
God helps you out or answers your
prayers, do you tell people about it?

It's easy not to notice when God is
working in our lives. But we should
look out for it, and praise Him when
He does.

And we can tell our friends all
about it!

What happened
with that hassle
at home?

Well, er, I
talked to God
about it and an
amazing thing
happened...

Action!

Look for opportunities to give God
the glory. When you see God at
work in your life, see if you can slip
it into your conversation.

Pray!

Think of three great things you
can praise God for.
Then ask Him to help you
mention them in your everyday
conversations.

Empires strike back

**Daniel
2 v 31-43**

At last!

Today we finally find out what the king's dream was and what it means.

WEIRD WORDS

Chaff
Hard stuff around wheat that is thrown away

Threshing-floor
Where chaff is removed from wheat

Dominion
Authority

Brittle
Weak and likely to break

Read Daniel 2 v 31-35

Nebuchadnezzar dreamed of a huge and awesome statue.

Fill in what the different parts of the statue were made of.

King Neb dreamed that a rock smashed the statue to pieces and the bits were blown away. But the rock became a huge mountain and filled the earth.

Daniel told the king what the statue was a picture of...

Cross out the wrong answers.

1. Read verses 36-38

The *gold/goat/grape* head is King Nebuchadnezzar and **Babylon**. He had huge power, but it was all given to him by **God** (v37). God is in control. King Neb was only powerful because God allowed him to be.

2. Read verse 39

The *shiny/silver/silly* chest and arms probably stand for the **Medes and Persians**. They would conquer Babylon but were not so powerful.

3. Read verse 39 again

The belly and thighs of *beauty/ bronze/bacon* are probably **Greece**, who would be the next nation to conquer the earth.

4. Read verses 40-43

Next, the **Roman empire** would take power and be as strong as *iron/Irene/iPad* (v40). But it would eventually split into small kingdoms, some weak (clay), some strong (iron).

God gave Nebuchadnezzar his dream 100s of years before most of these events happened. But it all came true — check the history books!

Pray!

Everything that has happened in history has happened according to God's plans. He's in control, not anyone else.
Thank God that He controls everything that *has* happened, *is* happening and *will* happen.

But what about the rock that smashed the powerful nations? What's that all about? Find out tomorrow in *Discover*...

Rock 'n rule

**Daniel
2 v 44-49**

Remember the king's dream?

Take a peek at yesterday's page if you need to.

WEIRD WORDS

Endure
Exist for ever

Fell prostrate
Fell flat on his face out of respect for Daniel

Incense
Powder burned to make a sweet smell

Lavished
Gave generously

Province
Large area of land, like a county or state

King Nebuchadnezzar dreamed of a huge statue. What four powerful nations was it a picture of?

B_____

M_____ and P_____

G_____

R_____

But in his dream the statue was smashed to pieces by a rock, and the rock grew into a massive mountain filling the whole earth!

Read Daniel 2 v 44-45

This rock stands for a kingdom that would destroy these great nations. How?

Because it was set up by the

G_____ of h_____

(verse 44)

The rock was the start of this great kingdom. The rock was actually a person that God sent to be King. But who was He?

Look up Luke 1 v 31-33

J_____

Wow!

Jesus is the King of the universe. He defeated God's enemies when He died and rose back to life. His kingdom will rule for ever! And all Christians are part of that awesome kingdom.

Read Daniel 2 v 46-49

The king was impressed. He was impressed with **Daniel**, gave him lots of prezzies and a powerful job in charge of many men. He even gave Daniel's friends top jobs too.

King Neb was also impressed with **God**. He saw that God is powerful and mighty and can even reveal dreams. But would the king live God's way? We'll find out tomorrow.

Think!

Praise and worship our amazing, powerful God as you pray. Thank Him for sending Jesus as the perfect King. Ask Him to help you live for Him.

21

Daniel 3 v 1-7

God has helped Daniel to explain the king's dream to him.

WEIRD WORDS

Plain of Dura
Wide open space

Satraps, prefects, governors etc.
Really important people

Dedication
Like an opening ceremony

Herald
The king's messenger

Zither
Instrument with strings

Lyre
Small harp

Bow now!

*Flick back to **Daniel 2 v 47** and complete what the king said.*

Fill in the vowels (aeiou) please.

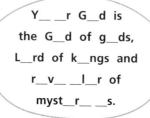

Y__ __r G__d is the G__d of g__ds, L__rd of k__ngs and r__v__ __l__r of myst__r__ __s.

But King Neb didn't worship God for long...

Read Daniel 3 v 1-7

Nebuchadnezzar built a huge gold statue. He then gathered all the most important people in the country and forced them to bow down and worship the statue. Anyone who refused would be thrown into a fire-filled furnace!

So they all bowed down to it. What an amazing scene — all these people worshipping a gold statue as tall as a 10-storey building! But they were doing a terrible thing.

Check out Exodus 20 v 4-6

That's one of the 10 Commandments. Fill in the vowels please.

You sh__ll n__t m__k__ an __m__g__ in the form of __nyth__ng in h__ __v__n above or the __ __rth beneath or the w__t__rs below. Y__ __ sh__ll n__t b__w d__wn to them or w__rsh__p them.

Read it through again. God commanded His people not to worship anything except Him. King Nebuchadnezzar and his people were going against God.

Wow!

God should come FIRST in our lives. We shouldn't worship anything else. NOTHING should be more important to us than God.

Pray!

Thank God that He's not a useless statue. Thank Him that He's real and with us all the time. Ask Him to help you worship Him by the way you live your life this week.

Tomorrow: will Daniel's friends worship the statue too?

22

**Daniel
3 v 8-18**

*King Neb has
commanded
that everyone
must bow down
to the golden
statue...*

*...or be thrown
into a giant
furnace.*

Stand up for God

Remember Daniel's three friends Hananiah, Mishael and Azariah? Along with Daniel they loved God and refused to eat the royal food. Now they're known as **Shadrach, Meshach and Abednego**, and they're in trouble...

Read Daniel 3 v 8-12

These cruel men snitched on Shadrach, Meshach and Abednego for not worshipping the statue. Sadly, God's people will often get hassled for obeying Him.

These days, if we stand up for God and refuse to sin, we won't get thrown into a furnace!

What might happen if you refuse to join in with stuff that's wrong?

_____

_____

_____

Think!

Do you stand up to the crowd despite what might happen to you?

Read verses 13-15

When King Neb heard about it he was furious! He tried to persuade them to go along with his law...

> **Just bow down
> and you'll be fine.**

Our friends sometimes try to persuade us to go against God...

> **Go on, do it, it
> won't do any harm!**

Read verses 16-18

What an amazing and brave answer! They knew God could save them from the flames (v17). But even if He didn't, they were determined to serve Him and not give in to sin (v18).

Pray!

What temptations do you face from friends and family?

_____

_____

_____

_____

Ask God to give you the strength and courage to stand up to the crowd and not give in to sin.

Tomorrow: facing the fire...

Facing the fire

**Daniel
3 v 19-30**

*Shadrach,
Meshach and
Abednego won't
bow down to the
golden statue.*

*They won't
disobey God even
if it means they'll
be thrown into a
furnace!*

Read Daniel 3 v 19-25

The furnace was like a big beehive-shaped chimney with a door at the bottom to put the wood in to be burnt.

Shadrach, Meshach and Abednego were thrown over the top while the king watched through the door.

*Now fill in the chart by using **verses 24-25**.*

Incredibly a man appeared in the furnace with them, freed them, and kept them from harm. God saved them from certain death!

What King Neb expected	What actually happened
3 men in the furnace	_____ men
Firmly tied up	
All 3 to be dead	

*Check out **Isaiah 43 v 2** and complete the sentence at the top of the page.*

When you walk through the fire

_____

_____

_____

_____

Wow!

That means when we stand up for God, He has promised to look after us. Even in countries where Christians get killed for their faith, they know that God will take them safely home to heaven! Whatever the bad situation is, He will be there with us!

Read Daniel 3 v 26-30

Because these men refused to sin, they were thrown into the furnace. But look what effect it had! Everyone saw how amazing God was. Even the king praised God. All because they refused to do wrong.

Even when people give us a hard time for living God's way, God can still be at work in their lives!

Pray!

Ask God to help you stand up for Him at school, even when it seems so hard. Pray that your actions would show people around you how great God is.

WEIRD WORDS

Unbound
No longer tied up

Son of the gods
Angel

Decree
Command

Saul: Israel's first king

24

**1 Samuel
8 v 1-9**

Today we're back in 1 Samuel.

The Israelites had been disobeying God.

But God put Samuel in charge of them. God was with them again!

WEIRD WORDS

Perverted justice
Twisted what was right and disobeyed God

Elders
Leaders

Forsaking
Abandoning

Solemnly
Very seriously

Samuel — the facts!

With Samuel in charge, life looked good for Israel. But major problems were ahead...

1. Samuel was getting old, and there was no one obvious to take over from him.

2. Samuel appointed his sons as leaders, but they were dishonest and sinful.

3. The Israelites were God's people, but they didn't want to serve God any more.

So who did they want to rule over them instead of God? Let's find out...

Read 1 Samuel 8 v 1-6

Fill in the gaps with the right words.

> prayed   old   happy
> Israelites   God   nations
> king   Samuel   Lord

The _____

thought that _____

was too _____ to lead them.

They were not _____

serving _____ and

demanded a _____ to

lead them. They wanted a

king because all the other

_____ had one.

Samuel was really upset.

So he _____ to

the _____.

Think!

Samuel took his problems to God. Do you turn to God in prayer when you see people going against Him?

Read verses 7-9

The Israelites were not just rejecting Samuel. By wanting a king to rule them, they were **rejecting God**. God was their King, the one who ruled them. Rejecting God was a really bad move.

Even though the people turned their backs on God again, He still listened to them! (v9)

Pray!

Thank God for His amazing love for you. Even though we let Him down so often, He never gives up on His people. Spend time praising God for who He is and what He's like.

Dare to be different

1 Samuel
8 v 10-22

The Israelites are not satisfied with God and want a king to rule over them.

So God gets Samuel to warn the people what having a king would mean for their lives.

Read 1 Samuel 8 v 10-18

Circle the ways that having a king would affect their lives.

> **Lose their daughters**
>
> **They'd become rich**
>
> **Sons would join the army**
>
> **Lose servants and animals**
>
> **Extra holidays**
>
> **Less work**
>
> **Lose the best wine and grain**
>
> **No more problems**
>
> **Become the king's slaves**

So having a king wouldn't be as great as they thought. Worst of all, they would cry out to God because of the way the king treated them. But God would not listen to them any longer (v18).

With a clear warning like that, surely Israel wouldn't want a king any more...

Read verses 19-20

The people ignored God's warnings. They wanted their own way.

Think!

Do you ever do that? Ignore what God says in the Bible? Not listen to what you're taught in Christian meetings? Go your own way instead?

The Israelites wanted to be the same as other nations. To fit in.

Think again!

Do you want to be the same as everyone else? To fit in? Or are you prepared to be different for God? To live a life that pleases Him, not anyone else?

Read verses 21-22

God was going to give them the king they wanted! Sometimes God lets us have our own way, so we learn that **His way is always the best way!**

Pray!

Say sorry for times you've ignored God and gone your own way. Ask God to help you obey Him, not go your own way. Ask Him to help you to be different for Him — to stand out as a Christian!

God calls tall Saul

26

**1 Samuel
9 v 1-17**

Saul

God is going to give His people the king they asked for!

But who will be Israel's first king?

WEIRD WORDS

Man of standing
Well respected

Quarter of a shekel
3 grams

Seer
God's messenger

Sacrifice
An offering (gift) for God

Anoint him
Pour oil on his head to show he has been chosen to serve God

Govern
Rule

Read 1 Samuel 9 v 1-4

... and fill in the fact file.

> **SAUL – THE FACTS!**
> **BACKGROUND**
> Son of K__sh (v1)
> From the tribe 0f B__
> nj__m__n (v1)
>
> **DESCRIPTION**
> T__ll and
> h__nds__m__ (v2)
>
> **JOB**
> D__nk__y herder! (v3)

Could this young donkey herder really become the king of Israel? But first things first, he's got to find his father's donkeys. And maybe bump into a prophet...

Read verses 5-10

Saul doesn't sound much like a leader. But God often has big plans for people who don't seem important or special. He can use the most unlikely people in the most incredible ways.

Who else has God chosen in this way?

M_____

(Exodus 3 v 1-4)

G_____

(Judges 6 v 15-16)

D_____

(1 Samuel 16 v 11-13)

Read verses 11-17

Saul was looking for donkeys but found Samuel instead. It was all part of **God's plan** (v15-17).

> **God heard the Israelites crying out to Him for a king. Saul would be the l__ __d__r of G__d's p__ __pl__ and would rescue them from the Ph__l__st__n__s (v16).**

God answered His people's cries and chose Saul to be king. God was in complete control of events.

Pray!

Thank God that...
• He is in control of everything.
• He hears our cries.
• He uses the most unlikely people to serve Him.

Oil for one

**1 Samuel
9 v 18 – 10 v 1**

Tall Saul was out looking for his dad's donkeys, but instead he found God's prophet...

Read 1 Samuel 9 v 18-27

Fill in the missing words. They can be found in the wordsearch.

Saul went to see

S_____, God's

prophet (v18). But Samuel

was already

ex_____

Saul, because God had told

him Saul was on his way.

Samuel told S_____

not to worry about the

d_____ as they'd

already been found (v20).

So Saul ate with Samuel.

Next m_____ they

walked together and Samuel

told Saul he had a special

m_____ for Saul

from God (v27).

WEIRD WORDS

Seer
Prophet, God's messenger

Desire of Israel
Israel wanted a king, and it would be Saul

Clan
Family

Anointed
Chosen you to be God's king

G	D	O	N	K	E	Y	S	S
O	G	N	I	N	R	O	M	A
D	M	E	S	S	A	G	E	U
I	S	I	N	C	O	N	T	L
L	E	U	M	A	S	R	O	L
E	X	P	E	C	T	I	N	G

Samuel told Saul he was special to Israel (v20). Saul couldn't believe it because he was from the smallest clan in the smallest tribe. But God often uses the weakest or least likely people to serve Him. So there's hope for people like you and me!

Read 1 Samuel 10 v 1

What's all that about?

Pouring oil on Saul's head was a sign that God had chosen him to be king. He would rule over the Lord's inheritance: that means the Israelites and their land. And he would have God's support.

Now write down the leftover letters from the wordsearch (in the same order).

___ ___ ___   ___ ___   ___ ___

___ ___ ___ ___ ___ ___ ___

It was **God** who brought Saul to meet Samuel.

It was **God** who chose Saul as king.

God was in control!

Pray!

God is always in control. How does that make you feel? Talk to God about it.

Answer: GOD IS IN CONTROL

Time of the signs

**1 Samuel
10 v 1-9**

Saul had set out to find his dad's donkeys.

Instead, he found out that he'd be Israel's new king!

WEIRD WORDS

Philistine outpost
Base of the evil Philistines

Prophets
Men who told people what God wanted to say to them

Lyres
Like harps

Prophesying
Here it means praising God

Samuel poured oil on Saul's head as a sign that he would be king of God's people, the Israelites (v1). God also gave Saul other signs to show that he would be God's king.

Read 1 Samuel 10 v 1-8

Number the events 1 to 7 in the order they would happen.

○ **Go to the tree of Tabor**

○ **Meet loads of prophets playing instruments and prophesying**

○ **They'll give you some bread**

○ **They will tell you the donkeys have been found**

○ **You'll receive the Spirit of the Lord and be changed**

○ **Meet two men near Rachel's tomb**

○ **Meet three men carrying wine, three goats and three loaves of bread**

Read verse 9

All of those things came true! They were so specific (unlike horoscopes!) that Saul knew that he really was God's chosen king.

Read verses 6-8 again

God gave Saul the Holy Spirit to help him serve God. And God would also instruct Saul how to serve Him. God would use Samuel to tell Saul what the Lord wanted him to do.

Wow!

God gives all His people (Christians) the Holy Spirit to help them to serve Him!

And He instructs them on how to live for Him. The Bible gives us loads of great advice on how we can serve God. We should read it and follow it.

Pray!

Read Psalm 32 v 8 and use it to praise God!

29

Saul singing, Saul dancing

**1 Samuel
10 v 10-19**

*God has chosen
Saul to be
Israel's king.*

Read 1 Samuel 10 v 10-13

Saul joined the prophets in praising God. This amazed the locals.

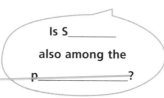

Is S_____

also among the

p_____?

They were so surprised to see Saul praising God that this became a catchphrase every time something unbelievable happened.

But someone wasn't so surprised.

Who is their

f_____?

Read verses 17-19

The L_____

rescued you from

E_____ and all the

k_____ that

oppressed you (v18). Yet you

have re_____ Him

and asked for a k_____

to rule over you instead of

G_____ (v19).

WEIRD WORDS

Prophesying
Praising God

High place
Where God was
worshipped

Kingship
Becoming king of
Israel

Delivered
Rescued

Oppressed
Treated really badly

Calamities
Disastrous situations

Clans
Families

That means *"God is their Father. He has caused this to happen"*.

Wow!

God often uses unlikely people to serve Him in amazing ways. And He gives them the ability to do it. God could even use you!

Read verses 14-16

Saul kept quiet about becoming king. (But the secret will be out in tomorrow's Discover...)

Even though God had done such amazing things for them, they didn't want Him to be in charge.

Pray!

Do you ever treat God like that? Spend time talking to Him about your answer.

**1 Samuel
10 v 20-27**

*God has chosen
tall Saul to be
the first king of
the Israelites.*

*But what will
the people
think of God's
choice?*

Rely on God

Read 1 Samuel 10 v 20-22

Samuel told the people that
God had chosen Saul to be their
king. But they couldn't find Saul
anywhere.

So what did they do? (v22) *Go back
one letter to find out... (B=A)*

— — — — —
B T L F E

— — —   — — — —
U I F   M P S E

They relied on God.

Think!

We must rely on God to help us
serve Him. Remember John 15 v 5?
(Look it up!)

We must stay connected to Jesus.
We can't live for Him without His
help.

Read verses 23-25

When the people found Saul, they
were impressed. He looked like a
king!

Then what did Samuel do?

— — — —   — — —
S F B E   P V U

— — — — —   — —
S V M F T   P G

— — — — — — —
L J O H T I J Q

Saul was **God's** chosen king, so
he had to obey **God's** rules. Even
though Israel had a king, **God**
would still be in charge.

Wow!

If you're a Christian, you're one of
God's people. He's in charge of
your life! You live for Him. And He's
given you His instructions in the
Bible to help you serve Him.

Read verses 26-27

Not everyone was pleased with
God's choice of king.

God's servants will always get
hassled by some people.

Action!

If you're serious about serving
God, try this: every morning, ask
God to help you serve Him that
day. Hand over all your worries
and problems to Him. Rely on
Him to help you.

WEIRD WORDS

By lot
Like flipping a coin

**Rights and
duties of
kingship**
Rules for being
God's king

Valiant
Very brave

31

**1 Samuel
11 v 1-11**

It's time for Saul's first challenge as king...

WEIRD WORDS

Ammonites
Enemies of Israel

Besieged
Surrounded with his army

Treaty
Peace agreement

Subject to you
Ruled by you

Spirit of God
Holy Spirit

Mustered
Gathered

Elated
Really really happy!

One in the eye

Read 1 Samuel 11 v 1-3

Jabesh Gilead was an Israelite town, so its people were God's people. Nahash and the Ammonites were a nasty bunch who wanted to invade the town. They wanted to gouge out the people's eyes (yeurggh!!) to disgrace God and His people.

Wow!

People will often try to disgrace and humiliate God and His people (Christians). But we can turn to God for help.

The people of Jabesh Gilead were ready to give up, but they sent out a desperate cry for help...

Read verses 4-5

What was the new king doing? Cross out all the As, Bs and Cs.

**A P L B O U C G H B A I N C C G
T A C H E B F I A E C L A D C C S**

— — — — — — — — —

— — —   — — — — — —

What could a mere farmer do to stop an enemy army?

Let's find out...

Read verses 6-11

Saul was furious. He made sure that all the Israelites knew they had to serve him. Then they attacked the Ammonites at night and slaughtered them.

What an amazing transformation! One minute Saul was a regular farmer, the next he was God's furious king leading God's people to victory over their enemies!

What made the difference (v6)?

**A T H C C E S B A P I C A R I B
B T O A B F G C C A O D B A C**

— — —   — — — — — —

— —   — — —

The **Holy Spirit** transformed Saul and helped him to serve God in an amazing way.

Pray!

On our own, we're useless! But the Holy Spirit helps us to live for God! Thank God for the fantastic gift of the Holy Spirit.

32

Celebration nation

**1 Samuel
11 v 12-15**

*The Israelites
have just had
their first victory
with Saul as
their king.*

They're so happy with their new king that they want to execute anyone who earlier criticised Saul (see 1 Samuel 10 v 27).

Read 1 Samuel 11 v 12-13

What did Saul say (v13)?

"Yeah, let's kill them!" ☐

"Just hurt them a bit" ☐

"No one shall be killed" ☐

Saul showed compassion and forgiveness for those who had doubted him. Just as God did with the Israelites when they'd turned their backs on Him.

Who did Saul say had really won the victory?

Saul on his own ☐

The Lord ☐

That guy with the big muscles ☐

Saul seemed to be the sort of king God wanted — one who obeyed God's Word and recognised it was God's victory. A promising start.

Read verses 14-15

What did the Israelites do? *(tick more than one)*

Confirmed Saul as king ☐

Broke down in tears ☐

Played beach volleyball ☐

Offered sacrifices to God ☐

Confirmed Saul as priest ☐

Had a huge celebration ☐

All the Israelites got together and gave their allegiance to King Saul. More importantly, they renewed their commitment to serving God.

WEIRD WORDS

**Renew
the kingship**
Confirm Saul as
their king

**Sacrificed
fellowship
offerings**
Gave offerings of
animals to God.
It showed
that they had
promised to serve
God and He had
promised to be
with them as
their God.

Pray!

Do you want to serve God? Then tell Him! Read through the prayer below. If you really mean it, read it to God.

Dear God, You are King of my life. I want you to have control of my life, and I want to serve you in everything I do. Please help me to live for you. Amen.

Write it out and stick it on your wall. You could pray it to God regularly.

Say it again, Sam

**1 Samuel
12 v 1-15**

*Uh-oh. Samuel
the prophet has
got a few things
to say to the
Israelites.*

WEIRD WORDS

Testify
Speak out

His anointed
God's chosen king
— Saul

Oppressed
Treated harshly

Forefathers
Ancestors

Righteous
Great, perfect

Forsaken
Abandoned

Read 1 Samuel 12 v 1-5

First off, Samuel let the people know
that he had served both God and
the Israelites well.

He'd never stolen any donkeys or
taken any bribes! But the people
hadn't behaved so well...

Read verses 6-13

*Fill in some of the great things God
had done for Israel.*

- **God sent M_____ and
  A_____ to rescue
  them from slavery in
  E_____ (v8)**
- **He heard the Israelites
  c_____ing out (v10)**
- **God sent Gideon, B_____,
  J_____
  and S_____ to
  rescue Israel from their
  e_____ (v11)**
- **He gave them the k_____
  they'd asked for (v13)**

*Despite God's great love and
kindness, what did the people do?*

- **They f_____ the
  Lord their God (v9)**
- **They started serving false
  gods like B_____ and
  A_____ (v10)**
- **They wanted a k_____
  to rule over them instead
  of G_____ (v12)**

Yet God didn't abandon His people!

Read verses 14-15

The Israelites now had a choice:

Serve
and obey
God and He
will be
with you

or

Turn
against
God and
He'll turn
against
you

Pray!

Ask God to help you choose the
first option and stick with it!
Remember the Pray! box from
yesterday? Want to read it to
God again?

Rain of thought

**1 Samuel
12 v 16-25**

*Old man Samuel
is telling the
Israelites off for
turning away
from God and
wanting their
own king.*

*And the Lord
is going to
do something
spectacular to
make them pay
attention...*

Read 1 Samuel 12 v 16-19

It never rained at that time of year!
The people realised how powerful
God was. He could easily destroy
them for rejecting Him. They realised
how badly they had treated God.
And they asked Samuel to pray
to God, asking Him not to punish
them.

Wow!

Our God is so powerful!
We've sinned against Him and
deserve His punishment. But He
is also so loving that He gives us
the chance to turn back to living
His way.

After realising how badly we've
treated God, what should we do?

Read verses 20-21

1. _ _ _ _ ' _ _ _ _

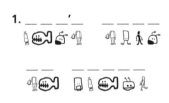

Don't put anything else before
God — friends, sport, school,
possessions. Serving God means
putting Him first in your life.

Read verse 22

2. Remember that

Cheer up! Even though we've
let God down, He still loves His
children! If you've had your sins
forgiven by God, He will never
leave you!

Read verses 23-25

3. _ _ _ _ _ _ _

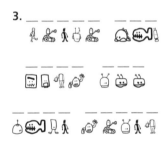

Serving God is more than going to
church and reading your Bible. It
means doing EVERYTHING for Him.
Whether you're doing schoolwork
or chatting with friends or shopping,
you should do it in a way that
pleases God.

**Ask God to help you to serve
Him in these three ways.**

WEIRD WORDS

Awe
Amazement

Idols
Fake gods. Idols can
be anything that is
more important to
us than God.

Fear the Lord
Respect Him

35

1 Samuel
13 v 1-15

Samuel has told King Saul and the Israelites to obey God.

Do you think they will?

WEIRD WORDS

Hebrews
Israelites

Obnoxious to the Philistines
The Philistines hated them!

Critical
Really bad

Thickets
Bushes

Cisterns
Wells

The Jordan
Big river

Endure
Continue

Saul slips up

Read 1 Samuel 13 v 1-4

Saul and his son Jonathan got an army together and attacked God's enemies, the Philistines. But Saul and his army were in for a shock...

Read verses 5-7

The Philistines had a MASSIVE army! The Israelites were scared stiff, and many ran away or hid.

But what had they forgotten? (Use yesterday's code.)

Read verses 8-9

Before a big battle, God's people would offer sacrifices to the Lord. It showed they trusted Him and wanted His help.

But only the priest (Samuel) was allowed to do it. Saul ignored God's instructions. He was in big trouble...

Read verses 10-15

God had told His people to serve Him and obey Him. But Saul disobeyed God's command. So God took away his family's right to rule Israel. Saul's sons would not lead Israel because Saul had disobeyed God's commands.

Pray!

The Bible tells us how we can serve God and obey Him. Write down two ways you've disobeyed God...

_____

_____

_____

_____

Say sorry to God and ask Him to help you stop doing these things and obey Him more.

Want a free e-booklet on how to stick at being a Christian?
Email
discover@thegoodbook.co.uk
or check out
www.thegoodbook.co.uk/contact-us
to find our UK mailing address.

1 Samuel
13 & 14

King Saul is up against the massive Philistine army.

Most of the Israelites are scared and are hiding or have run away.

And things were about to get worse for the Israelites...

WEIRD WORDS

Detachments
Groups

Ploughshares, mattocks, axes, sickles
Farming tools

Ephod
Priest's clothes

Uncircumcised men
Enemies of God and the Israelites

Jon joins in

Read 1 Samuel 13 v 16-23

... and fill in the missing words.

None of Saul and Jonathan's soldiers had sw_____ or sp_____ (v22)!

How could the Israelites fight the huge Philistine army without swords or spears?!

Read 1 Samuel 14 v 1-5

King S_____ and his men sat under a t_____ (v2). They were probably too scared to fight. Saul's son J_____ was brave. He and another soldier went alone to the Ph_____ camp.

What is Jonathan doing?! Surely he'll get himself killed!

Read verses 6-10

Jonathan trusted the L_____ to help him. He knew that n_____ could stop God from s_____ His people (v6).

Jonathan knew that if God was on his side, then he'd be alright.

Read verses 11-14

Jonathan knew that the L_____ would give him victory (v12). Jonathan and his armour carrier defeated tw_____ Philistines (v14)!

Jonathan took a big risk and attempted a dangerous climb into enemy territory. But God was with him, protecting him and giving him strength. Unlike Saul, Jonathan showed his faith in God and God gave him victory!

Pray!

We can't do great things for God by ourselves, but we have God to help us! Thank Him that He is always there to help His people. Maybe there is something you need to ask God's help with right now...

37

Philistine fear

**1 Samuel
14 v 15-23**

Jonathan

*God has helped
Jonathan and his
armour-carrier
to climb into the
Philistine camp
and defeat loads
of Philistines.*

*Today's missing words can be
found in the Bible verses and in the
wordsearch.*

```
P A N I C C U L U A S
B H F A E O B I V X H
K I I Y J N T S D O A
V J G L D F J R N H K
I A P H I U B A U I E
C H I L L S A E O D L
T G R N S I T L R I K
O G O D E O T I G N F
R C M Z T N L T N G N
Y O Q V D P E E B E X
R S S D R O W S M Q S
```

Read 1 Samuel 14 v 15-19

G_____ caused the

g_____ to s_____

and the P_____

started to p_____

(v15). But S_____ didn't

recognise that God was

giving them v_____.

So he got A_____ the

priest to ask God what to

do (v18). He didn't realise

that God was already

helping them!

Think!

Do you recognise when God is at
work in your life? Do you thank Him
when He answers your prayers?

Read verses 20-23

Finally Saul and his men

went into b_____

(v20). The Philistines were in

total c_____,

attacking each other with

s_____ (v20). Many

of the l_____

who'd been h_____

in the h_____ joined the

battle (v22).

So who won the victory? (v23)

[   ]

Despite the fact that Saul was
useless and the Philistines were
mighty, the Lord rescued Israel.

Pray!

Thank the Lord that He does
amazing things in our lives, even
when we're useless.
Give Him the praise He deserves
for prayers that He has answered.

WEIRD WORDS

**Muster the
forces**
Gather the army

Ark of God
Special wooden box
that was a sign that
God was with His
people

Tumult
A confused riot

Hebrews
Israelites

38

**1 Samuel
14 v 24-52**

*Quick, do some
eye exercises!*

*We've got loads
to read today.*

WEIRD WORDS

Oath
Promise

Plunder
Stuff they'd taken
from the Philistines

Broken faith
Let God down

Altar
Where sacrifices to
God were offered

Cast lots
Throw dice to make
a decision

Deliverance
Rescue

Honey business

Read 1 Samuel 14 v 24-30

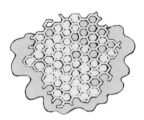

Even though they'd just fought a
battle, King Saul said that his troops
couldn't eat any food until the
evening. They were exhausted and
starving! But Saul's son Jonathan
broke the promise and ate some
honey.

Read verses 31-37

God had told his people not to
eat meat with blood still in it (see
Genesis 9 v 1-4).

So these soldiers were disobeying
God. Saul got the soldiers to offer
sacrifices to the Lord to say "sorry".
But when Saul asked God to help
him, God wouldn't answer because
the people had disobeyed Him.

Read verses 38-46

More bad decisions by King Saul.
He almost killed his son Jonathan
— the one who God had used to
rescue Israel from the Philistines!
But the soldiers wouldn't let Saul
kill Jonathan.

Saul didn't seem to be the perfect
king the people wanted.

Read verses 47-52

> **Saul and the Israelites
> had great victories over
> M_____, E_____,
> Z_____, the
> Amm_____, the
> Ph_____ and
> the Ama_____.**

Despite Saul letting God down, the
Lord continued to give Saul victory
over his enemies!

Pray!

Thank God that He uses weak,
sinful people like us in His plans!
Ask Him to help you to obey Him
more.

Destruction instruction

1 Samuel
15 v 1-11

Instructions for setting up your games console

1. Connect green lead to purple socket in TV
2. Press the big black button twice
3. Attach orange doobry to red thingummybob
4. Now play your shiny new games

Are you any good at following instructions? They're usually quite straightforward. But if you ignore them, you could end up blowing up your games console.
Or worse...

Over the last few days, we've seen how King Saul regularly failed to follow God's instructions. Now God has another task for Saul and the Israelites.

Read 1 Samuel 15 v 1-3

What were God's instructions?
Fill in the missing vowels (v3).

1. __tt___ck the
   __m__l_k__t_s
2. D__str__y __v__ryth__ng
   that b__l__ngs to th__m

The evil Amalekites had attacked God's people and so God was rightly punishing them. And He wanted Saul to do the business.

Read verses 4-9

> **Saul and the Israelites**
> __tt__ck__d the
> __m__l_k__t_s (v7).
> But they kept K__ng
> __g__g alive (v8). And they
> kept the b__st c__ttl__,
> sh__ __p, c__lv__s
> and l__mbs (v9).

In other words, Saul **DISOBEYED** God again.

Read verses 10-11

Saul had turned away from the Lord, and this deeply upset God.

Think!

Is there anything you keep from God (time, money, prayer)?

_____

_____

_____

Pray!

Say sorry to God and ask Him to help you give more of your

_____ to Him.

40

1 Samuel 15 v 12-23

Saul has disobeyed God by refusing to destroy all of the Amalekites and their animals.

WEIRD WORDS

Lowing
Mooing

Burnt offerings
Cooked meat given to God

Heed
Listen and obey

Rebellion
Turning against God

Divination
Using witchcraft and magic to make decisions

Idolatry
Worshipping fake gods

Saul's sly lies

Read 1 Samuel 15 v 12

Saul just gets worse! Now he's set up a monument to himself. That goes against one of God's 10 Commandments! (Exodus 20 v 4-6). And he's about to break another one...

Read verses 13-21

Spot Saul's lies.

1. I've obeyed the Lord's __nstr__ct__ __ns (v13).
2. We kept the best sh__ __p and c__ttl__. But not for ourselves! They were to s__cr__f__c__ t__ th__ L__rd (v15).
3. I d__d __b__y th__ L__rd! (v20)
4. I c__mpl__t__ly d__str__y__d th__ __m__l__k__t__s (v20)!

Pray!

Ever tried to cover up your tracks with lies and excuses? Say sorry to God for any lies you've told recently.

Read verses 22-23

Now fill in Samuel's response to Saul's lies.

It is better to __b__y G__d than to give him s__cr__f__c__s (v22). You've r__j__ct__d G__d's c__mm__nds, so the L__rd r__j__cts you as His k__ng (v23).

Saul continued to disobey God, so God would no longer support Saul as king. (More about that tomorrow...)

Pray again!

What really pleases God is when we obey Him. When we live our lives for Him. When we obey what we read in the Bible. Ask the Lord to help you to obey Him and serve Him this week.

That's torn it

**1 Samuel
15 v 24-35**

King Saul disobeyed God and then tried to cover it up with lies.

Do you think he's sorry?

WEIRD WORDS

Violated
Disobeyed

Hem
Edge of his robe

Glory of Israel
A name for God. Israel should be proud to have Him as their God.

Mourned
Was really upset

Read 1 Samuel 15 v 24-25, 30

Saul said that he was sorry. But he seemed to care more about what people would think if God's prophet Samuel left him.

Think!

Spend time asking God to be with you, helping you to grow into someone who serves Him with your whole life.

Read verses 26-34

How did God punish Saul for disobeying and rejecting Him? Cross out the Js, Qs and Xs.

TJHEQXLOQJRDHXJAST
QQQORNTJHEKXINGJDQ
OMOXQFISRJJAEQLAW
XJAYFQJROXXMYOQUJ

The_____
_____
_____
_____ (v28)

God was going to choose a new king (David) who would actually serve Him (v28). And God wouldn't change His mind (v29).

Wow!

God isn't soft. He punishes people who reject Him and refuse to live for Him. But that doesn't mean He's unloving...

Read verse 35

TXHELJQORDWQJASS
OXXRRJYTHJXATHQQE
HAXDMAJJDESAQJUL
KIXXNGOFISQJRAEQL

The_____
_____
_____
_____

Wow!

God wants us to be His friends and put Him first. God is upset when people reject Him and refuse to live for Him.

But it's not all sad news! When we come back to 1 Samuel (Day 63) we'll see God's new king, **David**, in action — serving God!

Pray!

If you mean it, say SORRY to God for specific times you've let Him down.

42

Jesus: Perfect teacher

**Luke
19 v 1-10**

Today we're jumping into Luke's book about Jesus.

Something BIG is about to happen to a little man!

Zacchaeus was a short guy. He was also a tax collector. He was a hated man because he overcharged people and kept some of the money for himself.

Read Luke 19 v 1-4

*Zacchaeus cheated people out of money. Write out the **CAPITAL LETTERS** to find a good thing about Zacchaeus.*

H E W t h A S e s D E e T l e t t
E R e r M I N s d o E D n t s p T O e
l l S E a E n y J E S t h i U S n g

H__ __ __ __

__ __ __ __ __ __ __ __ __

__ __   __ __ __

__ __ __ __ __

Think!

How determined are you to know more about Jesus? Do you just give up if the sermon is too hard or the Bible reading doesn't make sense?

Action!

Like Zacchaeus, don't give up! Ask God to help you understand. Ask an older Christian to help you. Don't give up until you get to know Jesus better!

Read verses 5-8

Circle the phrases that describe Zacchaeus after he'd met Jesus.

money-grabbing   **honest**

concerned about others

believing   **selfish**

generous   **dishonest**

Read verses 9-10

Jesus came to save people from their sins. He wants to make each of us one of God's people, so that our sins are forgiven and we give up our sinful ways.

Think!

Have you trusted Jesus to forgive your sins? In what ways has it changed your life? Do you need to change other things about the way you live?

Pray!

Now tell God how you feel and ask Him to help you out.

WEIRD WORDS

Jericho
City 15 miles from Jerusalem

Sycamore-fig
Strong tree, easy to climb

Salvation
Rescue from sin

Son of Abraham
One of God's people

Son of Man
Jesus

43

Luke
19 v 11-27

Time for a story from Jesus...

What can you do?

Read Luke 19 v 11-19

In the story, the king went away and left his servants with some of his money to look after.

JESUS is the man who has gone away (to heaven). And one day He's coming back. He will want to know what we have done with the **abilities** He has given us.

Which coins show ways we can use our abilities for God?

Wow!

What we do as we wait for Jesus to return does matter! People who don't use their abilities to serve God, but live for themselves, are in BIG TROUBLE when He returns.

WEIRD WORDS

Parable
Story told by Jesus to explain a BIG truth

Noble birth
Born into an important family

Ten minas
One mina was three months' wages

Delegation
Group of people

Reap
Collect crops

On deposit
In the bank

With interest
Extra money given by the bank

Wow!

God has given us all different abilities. He wants us to use these abilities to serve Him. One day He will reward us!

Read verses 20-27

This man did nothing with the money he was given. He was lazy and selfish and hid it. So the king punished him and also punished everyone who had turned against the King.

Action!

What can you do to serve Jesus at home, school and church?

_____

_____

_____

_____

Will you use those talents to serve God? Talk to Him now and ask Him to help you do it.

**Luke
19 v 28-40**

If you want to make a great entrance, you show up in something like a Ferrari.

But that's not the kind of entrance Jesus made in Jerusalem...

What an entrance!

Thousands of people were travelling to Jerusalem to celebrate the most important event of the Jewish year — the Passover festival.

But for Jesus, going to Jerusalem would mean so much more. Check out **Luke 18 v 31-33**.

For Jesus, the road to Jerusalem was also the road to His death.

Read Luke 19 v 28-36

Why did Jesus want a donkey?!

Check out what the prophet Zechariah said 500 years earlier. Read Zechariah 9 v 9 and fill in the missing vowels (aeiou).

R__j__ __c__,
Daughter Z__ __n!
Sh__ __t, Daughter
J__r__s__l__m! See, your
k__ng comes to you,
righteous and
v__ct__r__ __ __ s,
l__wly and r__d__ng
on a d__nk__y.

Read Luke 19 v 37-40

See how Zechariah's words came true? The crowds went wild for Jesus!

What did they call Jesus (v38)?

The k__ng who
c__mes in the n__m__
of the L__rd

Wow!

They were right that Jesus was their King who had come to save them. But they thought He would save them by fighting the Romans. They didn't realise that Jesus had come to die on the cross to save them from their sins.

A few days later, a crowd would be shouting for Jesus to be killed.

Pray!

Spend time praising King Jesus. Thank Him that He came as King to save His people from sin and punishment in hell.

Tears, temples & tricks

Luke 19 v 41 – 20 v 8

Loads more to learn from Jesus today...

Read Luke 19 v 41-44

Jesus knew that God was going to punish Jerusalem and destroy it. *What had the people done wrong? Go forward 2 letters (A=C, B=D Y=A etc) to find out.*

You didn't recognise the time

of _ _ _'_
    E M B Q

coming to _ _ _
           W M S

Jesus is God. He came to rescue these people from their sinful ways. But they **rejected** Him. That's why God would punish them.

Next stop, the temple. Where people went to meet God. But some people were only there to make money. Dishonestly.

Read verses 45-48

What did Jesus say the temple should really be?

— — — — — — — —
F M S Q C   M D

— — — — — —
N P Y W C P

Read Luke 20 v 1-2

Tricky question! If Jesus answered: *"I'm doing this by God's authority"*, they would probably kill Him.

And if He said: *"No one has given me authority to do it"*, He'd be shown to be a liar.

So Jesus asked them a tricky question instead. Clever, eh?

Read verses 3-8

They fell into their own trap!

If they said John's work was from God, they'd be admitting that Jesus came from God too. But if they said that John the Baptist hadn't been doing God's work, then they feared the people would turn against them.

WEIRD WORDS

Embankment
Tall structure to attack from

Hem you in
Surround you

Temple courts
Area outside the temple

Good news
The good news about how people can get right with God

Prophet
God's messenger, telling people what God wanted to say to them

Pray!

Ask God to help you to worship Him and talk to Him when you're at church. Ask Him to make it real to you, and not just a boring ritual.

Think & pray!

Who do you think Jesus is?

_____

_____

Will you thank Him for it?

46

**Luke
20 v 9-19**

*Jesus is telling
another
parable to the
unbelieving
Jewish leaders.*

WEIRD WORDS

Vineyard
Where grapes are
grown

Tenants
People renting the
vineyard

Heir
The son who would
inherit the vineyard

Cornerstone
The most important
stone in a building

Vine sign

Read Luke 20 v 9

The vineyard is a picture of **God's
people** (the Israelites). The owner
wanted fruit in his vineyard. It's
like God looking for fruit from His
people — expecting them to love
and obey Him.

Read verses 10-12

The owner sent s_____

to collect his fruit.

In the Old Testament, God sent His
servants (prophets) to tell His people
to start obeying Him again. But the
people ignored God's servants and
pleased themselves.

Read verses 13-15

Finally, the owner sent his son.
What happened to him?

_____

_____

_____

God sent His only Son, Jesus, to the
Israelites. *Did they listen to Him?*

YES/NO _____

Instead, they wanted to kill Him.

Read verse 16

The owner would kill the tenants
and give the vineyard to someone
else. Strong stuff, but they deserved
to be punished.

In the same way, God was
disappointed and angry with His
people when they murdered His
own Son, Jesus. Eventually they
were punished too.

God's message of forgiveness
through Jesus went to other people
and other nations.

Read verses 17-19

The cornerstone (v17) is the most
important stone — yet the builders
rejected it!

**Jesus is the most important
person ever! Don't reject Him
like these people did. God will
punish everyone who rejects
Jesus (v18).**

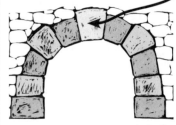

Pray!

Thank God for sending His own
Son Jesus to earth for us. Ask
Him to help you believe the truth
about Jesus and not reject Him.

A tax attack

**Luke
20 v 19-26**

The religious leaders are plotting to kill Jesus. They are trying to trick Him into trouble.

WEIRD WORDS

Governor
Local ruler

Sincere
Really meaning it

Partiality
Favouritism

In accordance
Agreeing

Caesar
Roman emperor

Duplicity
Deceiving ways

Denarius
Roman coin

Inscription
Writing

Read Luke 20 v 19-22

Rearrange the words to spell out the trick question.

pay   not?   Is
taxes   to   or   it
to   Caesar   us
for   right

Is _____
_____
_____
_____?

If Jesus said...

YES	NO
They could accuse Him of siding with the hated Romans against the Jewish people.	They could accuse Him of rebelling against the Romans and breaking the law by not paying tax.

How did Jesus answer?

Read verses 23-26

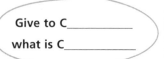

Give to C_____
what is C_____

Wow!

We must pay taxes and obey the government's laws. The Bible says we should obey the laws of the country we live in.

But what else?

Give to G_____
what is G_____

Wow!

God created us, so we should give our lives to Him, obeying and serving Him. We should live our lives for God.

Action!

How will you give to God what belongs to Him?
a) spend time talking to Him
b) obey what you've read in the Bible
c) show love to people you find it hard to love
Now ask God to help you!

48

Luke 20 v 27-40

Remember the tricky question Jesus had to answer yesterday?

Today He faces another one...

WEIRD WORDS

Resurrection
Coming back to life. Here it means eternal life with God.

Account of the burning bush
When God spoke to Moses from a burning bush. It's in Exodus 3 v 1-6.

Sad you see?

This time it's the **Sadducees** trying to catch Jesus out.

They were rich Jews who didn't believe in life after death. They hated the Pharisees, but hated Jesus even more.

Read Luke 20 v 27-33

It doesn't seem very likely, does it? One woman marrying **SEVEN** brothers, one after the other?!

But the Sadducees thought this bizarre question would beat Jesus. They even quoted Moses (v28). Surely Jesus couldn't get out of this one...?

Think again!

Read verses 34-36

Jesus didn't waste much time with the Sadd' guys' question.

Wow!

Eternal life won't be the same as life here on earth! In eternity we'll have brand new bodies. And we won't be married. There will be something far better!

Read verses 37-40

Jesus had a puzzle for the Sadducees. If they said there was no life after death...

Why did God say that He <u>IS</u> the God of A_____,
I_____ and
J_____? They'd all been buried for ages!

Read verse 38 again
God is not the God of the d_____ but of the
l_____.

Wow!

Abraham, Isaac and Jacob are still alive and with God! They were God's people so they went to live with Him when they died. When Christians die, they go to live for ever with God!

Pray!

Thank God that His people (Christians) will live with Him for ever!

Loads of lessons

49

Luke 20 v 41 – 21 v 4

Three big lessons from Jesus today!

LESSON 1: Jesus is God!

Jewish people were waiting for the Messiah (Christ) to come and rescue them. Jesus claimed to be the Messiah, but the teachers of the law knew the Messiah would be related to King David (v41). So they didn't believe He would be God too.

Read Luke 20 v 41-44

Here's what verses 42-43 mean...

It's something King David wrote in Psalm 110.

By calling the Christ **my Lord**, David is saying that the Messiah (Jesus) is also **God**. But the Jewish leaders hadn't worked that out.

LESSON 2: Watch out for dishonest leaders

Read verses 45-47

Shade in the boxes that describe these religious leaders.

Greedy	Humble	Honest
Show offs	Kind	Put others first
Selfish	Hypo-crites	Proud

People who serve God are like the boxes you didn't shade in.

LESSON 3: Give your best to God

Read Luke 21 v 1-4

Rich people had stacks of cash.

It didn't hurt them to give away their money. They had heaps left.

The widow gave everything she had, because she loved God and wanted Him to be first in her life.

Action!

Write down what you can give or do for God. Money? Time? Work? Be specific.

_____

_____

_____

Don't give God leftovers, give Him your BEST!

Pray!

1. Praise and thank Jesus that He is God!
2. Ask God to help you not listen to people who only pretend to serve Him.
3. Ask Him to help you with the stuff you wrote down under Action!

King of the hassle

50

**Luke
21 v 5-19**

*It's the end of
the world as we
know it...*

WEIRD WORDS

Adorned
Decorated

Uprisings
Fighting against
your country's
government

Pestilences
Nasty diseases

Persecute
Hassle you for
following Jesus

Adversaries
Enemies

Contradict
Prove wrong

Read Luke 21 v 5-11

Jesus said that the temple in Jerusalem would be destroyed (it was, only 40 years later). But He was also talking about what would happen before **the end of the world**, when Jesus will come back.

Before Jesus comes back, there will be wars (v9) and natural disasters (v11). And we need to watch out for people falsely claiming to be Jesus (v8). He gives us some more advice too...

Read verses 12-19

Now fill in the vowels (aeiou).

**1. Christians will be
   p__rs__c__t__d (v12)**

In some countries (like Turkey, Sudan and Algeria), Christians are attacked or arrested for following Jesus. That may not happen to us, but we should be ready to tell anyone about Jesus, whoever they are (v15).

2. Don't w__rry about it (v14) because God will give us the w__rds and w__sdom (v15) to tell people about Jesus!

God has given His Holy Spirit to all Christians, to help them live for Him. The Spirit helps us to tell people about Jesus. Whether it's in front of kings, judges or friends at school.

3. Everyone will h__t__ Christians because of Jesus (v17). But by st__nd__ng f__rm we will gain l__f__ (v19).

If you tell people about Jesus, expect to get lots of hassle. Even from your family and friends. But those who stand by Jesus to the end will live with Him for ever!

Pray!

1. Ask God to help Christians who are arrested or attacked for following Jesus.
2. Ask God to help you tell people about Jesus.
3. Thank God that He has promised to help you do it.
4. Ask God to help you stand up to any hassle you get for loving Jesus.

51

Luke
21 v 20-38

Wait for it...

Jesus is telling His disciples about the destruction of Jerusalem. And also about the end of the world. Scary stuff!

Read Luke 21 v 20-24

Cross out the sentences that don't fit the verses.

There's plenty of time
There's no time left
I'll just go back for...
Run to the mountains!
Help!

That's what happened when Jerusalem was destroyed by the Romans. But there won't be a chance to escape when Jesus comes again...

Read verses 25-27

How will Jesus return?

_____

_____

_____ (v27)

That's completely different from the way Jesus came into the world the first time — as an unknown baby sleeping in an animal trough. This time everyone will know that He is the **King of Kings**.

What should Christians do when Jesus comes back?

Read verse 28

We can look up in hope and joy because Jesus will rescue believers from their sinful lives and take them to live with Him for ever!

Read verses 29-33

We need to be ready for when Jesus returns. It could happen any time. So we should be living for God and telling people about Him right now!

Read verses 34-38

Jesus tells us not to doubt that He'll return. We should be ready, living for Him.

Pray!

Thank Jesus that He will return in an amazing way.
Ask Him to help you serve Him while you're waiting!

WEIRD WORDS

Desolation
Destruction

Fulfilment
What the prophets said is coming true

Wrath
God's anger

Gentiles
Non-Jews

Anguish
Fear and worry

Perplexity
Confusion

Apprehensive
Worried about

Heavenly bodies
Stars and planets

Redemption
Rescue

Carousing
Bad living

Anxieties
Worries

Daniel: Walk God's way

Daniel
4 v 1-3

Today we come back to daring Daniel's story.

Need a reminder of what's happened so far?

King Nebuchadnezzar captured some of the brightest young men in Jerusalem and took them back to Babylon.

Daniel and his friends stood out because they wouldn't eat the royal food. God made them better than all the other students.

God helped Daniel to interpret King Neb's dream, so the king put Daniel in charge of loads of people.

Daniel's friends (Shadrach, Meshach and Abednego) refused to worship a gold statue so they were thrown into a furnace. But God kept them alive and everyone saw how powerful God was!

Next, King Neb sent a letter to people all over the world…

Read Daniel 4 v 1-3

Something amazing happened to King Neb (we'll read about it over the next few days). He wanted to **tell everyone** what God had done.

Unjumble the anagrams to reveal what he said about God.

How g_____ are his
t a g e r

signs! How mighty are his

w_____! His
d o w n e r s

k_____ is eternal
m o k d i n g

and he shall rule for e_____!
r e e v

Nebuchadnezzar wanted everyone to know how great God is!

Think!

List some good things that have happened to you.

_____

_____

_____

_____

Do you tell everyone how great God has been to you?

Pray!

Do you thank God for what He's done for you? Now's a good time to start! Praise and thank Him for the things you've written down.

WEIRD WORDS

Prosper
Be successful

Eternal
It lasts for ever!

Dominion endures
God's power and authority will last for ever

53

**Daniel
4 v 4-18**

*We're reading
King Neb's
letter, telling
everyone how
great God is.*

WEIRD WORDS

**Contented and
prosperous**
Happy and successful

**Enchanters,
astrologers and
diviners**
Men who used dark
magic to advise the
king

Abundant
Loads of it

Times
Here it probably
means years

The Most High
God

Lowliest
Least impressive

Tree time

Read Daniel 4 v 4-8

King Neb had another nightmare.
Yet again, none of the wise guys
could tell him what it meant.

So he turned to Daniel (who he
called Belteshazzar).

Read verses 9-16

*Below, circle the words that describe
King Neb's dream.*

He dreamed about an enormou**s**/
ti**n**y/ug**l**y tree (v10). It was very
ol**d**/str**o**ng/purpl**e** (v11). Its lea**v**es/
branc**h**es/**a**pples were beautiful and
pe**o**ple/fi**s**h/b**e**asts sheltered under
it (v12). But an angel said the tree
must be cut down. Only the stump
and its fis**h**/fr**u**it/**r**oots would be left
(v15).

The tree in the dream represented
a p**e**rson/ani**m**al/cheese**c**ake (v16).
He would be cut down from his
powerful position and become like
an ani**m**al/anorak/**f**ish (v16). He had
to live among the plants and grape**s**/
grass/gra**v**y (v15) until si**x**/seve**n**/
ei**g**ht years had passed (v16).

*Now find today's key word. Take the
underlined letters from the words
you circled. Below, write them out
in the same order.*

God is

_ _ _ _ _ _ _ _

That means that God is in control of
EVERYTHING. He has the power to
do anything at all.

Read verses 17-18

Pray!

Thank God that He is sovereign —
that He's in control. If you mean
it, ask Him to rule YOUR life.

Tomorrow we'll find out what the
dream means and which person
these things will happen to...

Daniel dishes the dirt

**Daniel
4 v 19-27**

King Nebuchadnezzar dreamed about an amazing tree that was chopped down. Somehow, Daniel has to break it to King Neb that the tree represents him!

Read Daniel 4 v 19-22

Now fill in the missing verse numbers.

**The tree was so tall it could be seen all over the world
(verse _____)**

King Neb was known worldwide as a hugely powerful ruler.

**It had beautiful leaves and loads of fruit
(verse _____)**

King Neb's kingdom was rich, successful, and powerful.

**It fed and protected birds and animals
(verse _____)**

He had responsibility for all in his kingdom.

King Neb was the most powerful king in the world, ruling over many nations. But it wouldn't last...

Read verses 23-25

**Nebuchadnezzar would end up living like a wild animal, eating grass!
(verse _____)**

King Neb thought he was powerful and unbeatable. But God would show him who was really most powerful. Then the king would realise that it's **God** who is in control.

Read verses 26-27

**When Neb admits that God is in control, he'll get his kingdom back.
(verse _____)**

**Daniel told King Neb to give up his sinful ways and start treating people better
(verse _____)**

Tomorrow we'll find out if he took Daniel's advice.

WEIRD WORDS

Perplexed
Puzzled

Adversaries
Enemies

Dominion
Authority

Decree
Command

The Most High
God

Sovereign
In control of everything

Heaven rules
God is in charge of everything

Renounce
Give up

The oppressed
People who are treated badly

Think!

Jesus gives us the same warning: *"Unless you repent, you too will all perish"* (Luke 13 v 3). Have you turned your back on sin, to start living God's way?

55

Daniel 4 v 28-33

Before

Daniel told King Neb what his tree dream meant.

Flick back to yesterday's page if you need a reminder.

Would it come true?

Flick back to yesterday's page if you need a reminder.

WEIRD WORDS

Royal residence
City where the king lived

Majesty
Great power

The Most High is sovereign
God is in complete control!

Majesty to moo-sery

Read Daniel 4 v 28-30

King Nebuchadnezzar was so powerful. He built the beautiful city of Babylon with its famous Hanging Gardens, one of the **Seven Wonders of the World**.

But his success filled him with pride. He thought he was the best. But God was going to show him who was really in charge.

Read verses 31-33

It happened exactly as God had promised. King Neb was kicked out of Babylon and lived like a wild animal, eating grass.

He even started to look like an animal (v33)!

After

*To reveal what the Bible says about pride, take **every 2nd letter**, starting with the **top P**.*

(It's from Proverbs 16 v 18)

P _ _ _ _
_ _ _ _ _
_ _ _ _ _
_ _ _ _
_ _

Wow!

If we think we're in charge, rather than God, then one day we're in for a serious fall like King Neb. We must give God control of our lives, and live for Him.

Are you proud like King Neb?

Do you ever think or say...

- I'm so good at sport/school/ something else.

- I deserve more compliments from people.

- I don't need God to tell me what to do.

Pray!

Tell God about any times you've been proud. Say sorry and ask Him to forgive you.

Raised to praise

**Daniel
4 v 34-37**

Before

Yesterday we left King Neb nibbling on grass.

He'd been way too proud, so God showed him who was really in charge.

We've already seen Neb's fall...

From king of Babylon, admired by millions...

...to be like an animal, ridiculed by everyone.

Now we're going to see an even greater transformation...

Read Daniel 4 v 34-37

King Neb had praised God in the past, but then ignored Him. But this time he meant it.

It's no longer the fake words of a proud king, but the worship of a humbled sinner.

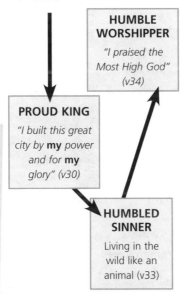

HUMBLE WORSHIPPER

"I praised the Most High God" (v34)

PROUD KING

*"I built this great city by **my** power and for **my** glory"* (v30)

HUMBLED SINNER

Living in the wild like an animal (v33)

King Nebuchadnezzar admitted that God was in control of everything, including his life. So God gave him his kingdom back.

After

When someone becomes a Christian, they go through similar stages to King Neb! Which one is most like you right now?

PROUD SINNER

You need to say sorry to God for the wrong things you've done. And you need to ask Him to forgive you.

HUMBLED SINNER

You've realised that you've let God down, but now you need to live your whole life for Him, putting Him first. Ask God to make you more like Jesus.

HUMBLE WORSHIPPER

Can you fill in your name with the rest of verse 37?

Now, I _____

praise and glorify _____

_____

_____

_____

WEIRD WORDS

Honour and splendour
All that he had before as king

Nobles
Important people

Exalt
Lift God up to be praised

Humble
Show them how weak they are

57

**Daniel
5 v 1-16**

*Now we jump
ahead a few
years. King Neb
is dead and now
King Belshazzar
is in charge.*

*But Daniel is
still around
somewhere...*

*(All of today's
missing words
can be found
down the centre
of the page. Fill
'em in!)*

WEIRD WORDS

Concubines
Women who
belonged to the
king

Insight
Understanding

Exiles
Men captured
from Jerusalem

Write and wrong

Read Daniel 5 v 1-4
King Belshazzar held a
b_____ for loads
of important people. He
had the special g_____
and s_____ goblets
brought to him. They were
from God's t_____
in Jerusalem. But they
drank w_____ from
them and praised false
g_____.

Read verses 5-9
Suddenly a h_____
appeared and started
w_____ on the
wall. The king turned
p_____ and his k_____
began to knock! He sent
for all the w_____ men,
but n_____ of them
knew what the
writing meant.

Read verses 10-16
The q_____ remembered
how D_____ had helped
King N_____.
She told Belshazzar and he
asked Daniel to r_____ the
writing to him.

banquet chain clothes Daniel gods gold hand knees Nebuchadnezzar none pale queen read ruler silver temple wine wise writing

He offered Daniel great
c_____, a gold
c_____ and the
job of third highest
r_____ in
the kingdom.

Belshazzar had used special
cups from God's temple to have
a drunken party and worship
idols! Once again, Daniel would
explain God's message to a
sinful king. It won't be good
news for the king!

Think!
Ever disrespected God? Told
wrong jokes? Made fun of
the Bible? Ignored Christian
speakers?

Pray!

Maybe you've been ungrateful
for things God has given you.
Or you've put other things first
instead of Him. Say sorry to God
for times you've shown disrespect
for Him.

Belshazzar's blunder

**Daniel
5 v 17-24**

King Belshazzar saw a ghostly hand write on the wall of his palace!

He offered Daniel loads of great things if he could read the writing.

WEIRD WORDS

Sovereignty
Great power

Splendour
Brilliance

Arrogant
Proud. Thought he was best.

Deposed
Removed

Acknowledged
Admitted

Read Daniel 5 v 17

Fill in the vowels to reveal Daniel's brave response to the king!

> You may k__ __p your g__fts and g__v__ your r__w__rds to someone __ls__. But I will still r__ __d the wr__t__ng for the k__ng and tell him what it m__ __ns.

Belshazzar had shown great disrespect for God, and had tried to buy Daniel's wisdom too. So Daniel bravely told him to shove it!

Read verses 18-21

What happened to King Neb?

> G__d gave King N__b__ch__dn__zz__r greatness and p__w__r over many n__t__ __ns. But King Neb became arrogant and pr__ __d, so God str__pp__d him of all his gl__ry. He was dr__v__n away from p__ __pl__ and given the m__nd of an __n__m__l.

God did all this to show that He was most powerful and in control of everything. Belshazzar knew this story, but what did he do?

Read verses 22-24

Belshazzar did not h__mbl__ himself. Instead he went against the L__rd of h__ __v__n. He misused the special g__bl__ts from God's t__mpl__, and pr__ __s__d false g__ds. He did not honour G__d, even though **God is in control of everything!**

Belshazzar knew all about God, yet he still worshipped false gods. We know loads about God from the Bible. We know He sent Jesus to rescue us from sin. And that if we refuse to trust Jesus, we'll be punished in hell. We've got no excuse for ignoring God!

Pray!

God graciously gives us time and opportunity to turn to Him. Have you done this or are you still saying "No" to God? How about your friends and family? Spend some time now praying for God's mercy.

59

Daniel
5 v 25-31

So what did the writing on the wall actually say? Tell me!!

OK, I get the message!

Let's find out...

Weight for it...

Read Daniel 5 v 25-28

> MENE, MENE,
> TEKEL, PARSIN

Complete the meanings below.

1. *Mene* means
n__mb__r__d (v26)

Belshazzar's days were numbered. He had sinned against God and God would punish him very soon.

2. *Tekel* means
w__ __gh__d (v27)

When measured against God's holy and perfect standards, Belshazzar had completely failed.

Think!

Belshazzar had lived his life in a way that was completely ignoring God.

But what about you?

You may not be as bad as Belshazzar, but does your life match up to God's standards?

> **Well, I go to church loads, I'm generous, I read my Bible and say my prayers and stuff...**

Even these things don't match up to what God requires of us.

The prophet Isaiah said that our good deeds are like filthy rags (Isaiah 64 v 6).

Even our best efforts are ruined by sin. They are as worthless as dirty bits of cloth. We desperately need Jesus to forgive us, or we too will be weighed and found to be no good.

3. *Parsin* means
d__v__d__d (v28)

Belshazzar's kingdom of Babylon was going to be divided. It would be taken over by the Medes and Persians.

Read Daniel 5 v 29-31

God's message to Belshazzar came true that night! Belshazzar got exactly what he deserved.

Pray!

Thank God that...
a) He's in control.
b) He keeps His promises.
c) He sent Jesus to rescue us from the punishment we deserve.

WEIRD WORDS

Reign
Rule as king

Medes and Persians
The countries of Media and Persia, Babylon's enemies

Slain
Killed

60

Roaring to go

**Daniel
6 v 1-14**

*King Neb's
gone, King
Belshazzar's
dead. The
next king is
Darius. And
no, he doesn't
live God's way
either...*

WEIRD WORDS

Satraps
Local rulers

Corruption
Law-breaking

Negligent
Careless

Prefects
Officials in charge
of people

Edict/decree
Order

Repealed
Cancelled

Read Daniel 6 v 1-4

King Darius was so impressed with
Daniel that he wanted to put him
in charge of everyone! This made
other important people jealous and
they looked for a reason to get rid
of him.

*Go back one letter to reveal what
they found out.*

E B O J F M   E J E

O P U I J O H

X S P O H

Think!

What things might people find
in your life? Lies? Teasing? Not
respecting your parents?

_____

_____

_____

We need to live God's way as much
as we can. So people see that He's
most important to us.

Read verses 5-9

It was a clever and evil plan.

They knew Daniel wouldn't stop
praying to God, and so he would be
thrown into the lion pit.

Read verses 10-14

What did Daniel do?

Q S B Z F E   U P

H P E   U I S F F

U J N F T

B   E B Z

Wow!

Obeying God must come first,
whatever the consequences. Is
prayer so important to you that
nothing would make you stop
talking to God?

Think & pray!

Any ideas how you can stand up
for your faith this week?

_____

_____

Ask God to help you do it!

61

Roaring success

**Daniel
6 v 15-23**

KEEP OUT!
LION PIT!

King Darius has been tricked into throwing Daniel to a pack of hungry lions.

Let's see what happened...

Read Daniel 6 v 15-18

King Darius didn't want to send Daniel to his death, but he couldn't get out of it. Daniel was thrown to the lions and a huge stone was put over the entrance so he couldn't escape.

King Darius was so worried about Daniel that he didn't sleep a wink all night. Was Daniel's God really powerful enough to stop these starving lions chewing him to pieces?

Read Daniel 6 v 19-23

Below, find the 5 sentences that are true. For each true sentence, circle the 2 letters next to it.

Daniel was safe because...

The lions weren't hungry	N O
God protected Daniel	T R
He had obeyed God	U S
He didn't look very tasty	N S
God's angel saved him	T E
The lions were asleep	E N
God controls everything, even lions	D G
Daniel was innocent in God's sight	O D
The lions were cuddly	S E

There is another reason why Daniel wasn't eaten. And it's also the reason why he hadn't been afraid to carry on praying to God.

To find it, copy out the letters you circled.

Daniel

_ _ _ _ _ _

_ _ _ (v23)

Daniel had refused to turn away from God. And he'd trusted God to look after him. So God kept him safe!

Wow!

Christians can expect to be hassled for serving God. But God is always with them, helping them and looking after them. That doesn't mean He'll always rescue us from a situation. But we can trust He's with us and that His perfect plans for us will work out.

Pray!

Thank God that He's always with His people. Ask Him to help you trust Him and stand up for Him.

WEIRD WORDS

Decree or edict
Command or law

Signet ring
Putting the mark of this ring on the stone meant that anyone who tried to rescue Daniel would be killed too

Anguished
Extremely worried

The living God

**Daniel
6 v 24-28**

*God brilliantly
saved Daniel
from being the
lions' next meal.*

*But what will
happen to the
bad guys who
set him up?*

Read Daniel 6 v 24

The evil plotters got what they
deserved. And their poor wives and
children were thrown in too. Daniel
had not been touched by the lions,
but these bad men were torn to
pieces before they hit the ground.
Everyone saw how powerful Daniel's
God was.

Read verses 25-28

King Darius told everyone how
awesome God was and that they
should all worship Him!

*Complete what Darius said about
God by finding the words in the
wordsearch.*

```
D Y F W O N D E R S
A E A R T H P C M A
N A S B D J G R Z V
I O G T H E V E R E
E L X K R L K S L S
L I O N S O U C T D
C V R P N M Y U V A
Q I E H E A V E N S
H N N E J O Q S D B
S G D K I N G D O M
```

He is the l_____ God.
He endures for e_____. His
k_____ will never be
d_____ and His
 power will never e_____.
He r_____ and He
 s_____. He performs
 miracles and w_____
in the h_____ and on
 the e_____.
He rescued D_____
 from the l_____.

Think!

Do you give God the praise He
deserves? And do you tell other
people how great He is?

Action!

Make a list of some of the great
things about God (check out
Psalm 65).

_____

_____

_____

WEIRD WORDS

Prosper
Be successful

Reverence
Show great respect

Endures
Lasts

Pray!

Now take time to praise and
thank God for the things you've
written about Him.

David: God's new king

**1 Samuel
16 v 1-13**

*Let's return to
the book of
1 Samuel.*

*King Saul kept
disobeying God.
So God rejected
Saul as His king.*

So would God let Israel fall apart?

Read 1 Samuel 16 v 1-3

God told the prophet Samuel to
stop sulking about Saul. Why?

Go back one letter to find out.

___ ___ ___ ___ ___ ___ ___ ___ ___
H P E   D I P T F

___ ___ ___ ___ ___ ___ ___ ___
B   O F X   L J O H

King Saul had rejected God. Yet
God didn't give up on His people,
the Israelites. He was going to give
them a new, better, godly king!

Read verses 4-7

Shocker! God didn't choose tall,
impressive Eliab. Why not? (v7)

___ ___ ___   ___ ___ ___ ___
U I F   M P S E

___ ___ ___ ___ ___   ___ ___
M P P L T   B U

___ ___ ___   ___ ___ ___ ___ ___
U I F   I F B S U

Wow!

How people appear on the outside
doesn't matter to God. He cares
about what we're like on the INSIDE.

Read verses 8-12

God chose Jesse's youngest, most
unlikely son to be the future king
of Israel. God often uses the most
surprising people in His plans!

Read verse 13

*What amazing thing happened
to David?*

___ ___ ___   ___ ___ ___ ___ ___ ___
U I F   T Q J S J U

___ ___ ___ ___   ___ ___ ___ ___
D B N F   V Q P O

___ ___ ___ ___ ___
E B W J E

God chose unlikely David to be His
king. And He gave David the Holy
Spirit to help him serve God.

The story continues tomorrow...

Pray!

Got anything you want to say to
God today?

WEIRD WORDS

Horn
Sheep's horn, used
like a jug!

Heifer
Young cow

Anoint
Pour oil on the head
of the one God
chose

Consecrate
Make pure by
washing

Harp of the matter

Hold on a minute! Surely King Saul's son Jonathan would become the next king. How could this ordinary, unknown shepherd boy take his place? It seems impossible.

Today we see the first small step towards David becoming king.

*Young David
has been
anointed — he
will become
king of Israel
one day.*

*David is God's
choice for king!*

Read 1 Samuel 16 v 14

Saul was in a mess. He had turned away from God, so God punished him by taking away the Holy Spirit from him — and by sending an evil spirit to bother him. But God can bring good out of even the worst situations.

Read verses 15-23

Fit the fact blocks into the grid in the order they happened.

Saul was told that David played the lyre

SAU

Saul sinned against God

DAV

David pleased Saul

LACE

Saul sent for David

L'S PA

An evil spirit tormented Saul

ID EN

1	2	3 Saul wanted a lyre player to relax him **TERED**
4	5	6

What do the CAPITAL LETTERS spell out?

D _____

_____

WEIRD WORDS

Evil spirit
We don't know exactly what this was. But we do know that God was in control of it (nothing is more powerful than God!). And we know that it upset Saul.

Lyre
Harp

Armour-bearers
Boys who carried the armour of important people

God's rejected king (Saul) has invited God's chosen king (David) into his palace! → God's plans for David to become king are starting to work out. → The impossible is beginning to happen!

Pray!

Thank God that His plans always work out — even when it seems impossible!

Little and large

Young David has been playing his lyre (harp) for King Saul. But now the scene changes...

WEIRD WORDS

Six cubits and a span
9 feet or 3 metres

5000 shekels
58 kilograms

Greaves
Leg armour

600 shekels
7 kilograms

Subjects
Slaves

Defy
Challenge

Ephrathite
Someone from near Bethlehem

Ephah
22 litres

Today's missing words can be found in the centre of the page.

Read 1 Samuel 17 v 1-11

The P_____ got ready to a_____ the Israelites. They camped at E_____ D_____.
King Saul and the Israelites camped in the Valley of E_____.
A huge man named G_____ challenged the I_____.
He was _____ tall, wore heavy a_____ and carried huge w_____.
He shouted: "If one of your m_____ fights and k_____ me, the Philistines will be your s_____. But if I win, you lot will be our s_____."
Saul and the Israelites were t_____.

Read verses 12-19

armour attack bread brothers cheese commander Dammim David eight Elah Eliab Ephes Goliath grain Israelites kills men Philistines Shammah sheep slaves subjects terrified weapons youngest 3 metres 9 feet

D_____ was the y_____ of Jesse's e_____ sons. His brothers E_____, Abinadab and S_____ all went to fight in the war. But David had to look after his dad's s_____. One day Jesse sent David to take g_____, b_____ and c_____ to his b_____ and their c_____.

Goliath and David were very different men. It's not surprising that the Israelites were terrified of Goliath. But flick back to **1 Samuel 16 v 7**. What we're like inside is far more important to God!

Pray!

Thank God that it doesn't matter how you look or what people think of you. Ask Him to change you on the inside so you serve Him with all your heart.

Giant steps

**1 Samuel
17 v 20-37**

No Israelite dares to fight Goliath the giant.

Meanwhile, David is leaving his sheep and taking supplies to his brothers in the army.

WEIRD WORDS

Defiance
Challenge

Exempt
Won't have to pay taxes

Uncircumcised
Enemy of God

Conceited
Self-centred and proud

Read 1 Samuel 17 v 20-24

David arrived just in time to hear Goliath's challenge and see the Israelites' fear.

Read verses 25-27

What three things would Saul do for the man who killed Goliath?

1.

2.

3.

But the reward wasn't the most important thing. What really bothered David? (v26)

> **That Goliath the ungodly Philistine was challenging the armies of the I_____ G_____**

David realised that Goliath was standing up to God Himself!

Think!

When people speak against God, do you stand up for Him? Or do you keep quiet because you're too scared?

Read verses 28-31

Eliab moaned like older brothers often do! But soon King Saul heard about brave David...

Read verses 32-37

Complete the three facts.

1. Goliath was a giant but David was only a y_____ (v33).

That's not important!

2. David had killed l_____s and b_____s (v36).

That's not important either!

3. David trusted that the L_____ would give him victory (v37).

THAT'S HUGELY IMPORTANT!

Pray!

Ask God to help you to trust Him more, and to always put Him first, as David did.

67

Giant killer

**1 Samuel
17 v 38-51**

*When a small,
unknown
soccer team like
Chesterfield
beats a huge,
successful team
like Manchester
United, they are
known as GIANT
KILLERS.*

*Guess where
that phrase
comes from!*

There was no doubt about who
the favourite was in this fight. King
Saul thought David needed all the
armour he could wear before facing
fierce Goliath.

Read 1 Samuel 17 v 38-44

David wouldn't even wear any
armour or carry a sword!

*Look at the verses from chapter 17
and fill in the stats.*

GOLIATH

• _____ tall (v4)
• Bronze h_____ (v5)
• Coat of a_____(v5)
• Bronze j_____(v6)
• Huge sp_____ (v7)
• And someone to carry his
  sh_____ (v7)

DAVID

• Only a b_____ (v42)
• No a_____ (v38-39)
• Just a s_____, five
  smooth st_____ and
  a sl_____ (v40)

Goliath was expected to smash
David to bits! But here are the more
important stats.

Read verses 45-47

GOLIATH

• Fought with a sw_____,
  a sp_____ and a
  j_____ (v45)

DAVID

• Fought with the L_____
  A_____ on his
  side! (v45)
• Wanted the whole
  w_____ to know
  that G_____ was with
  I_____ (v46)

Read verses 48-51

Huge Goliath had challenged God.
David fought for God's honour, and
God gave him an awesome victory!
This story is a picture of something
even more amazing — how Jesus
defeated sin and evil on behalf of his
people when he died on the cross.

Pray!

Thank God that He often uses
the weak to give Him glory! Ask
Him to help you to stand up for
Him the next time anyone speaks
against Him.

Friend or foe?

**1 Samuel
17 & 18**

King Saul congratulated David for defeating Goliath.

But Saul didn't know that God had chosen David to replace him as king.

Today's answers can be found in the verses and the wordsearch.

S	P	F	C	A	S	O	N	G	S
T	U	P	O	P	U	L	A	R	W
R	J	C	L	A	B	D	R	O	O
B	O	W	C	M	Z	N	M	K	R
U	N	S	B	E	L	T	Y	H	D
D	A	V	I	D	S	O	F	N	E
Q	T	K	L	U	A	S	G	E	H
L	H	V	R	X	P	Y	F	M	J
C	A	J	J	E	A	L	O	U	S
A	N	G	R	Y	B	Q	G	D	L

Read 1 Samuel 17 v 52 – 18 v 4

King S_____ was impressed with D_____ and always kept him close (v2). Saul's son J_____ became great friends with David (v3). He gave David his armour (tunic), s_____, b_____ and b_____ (v4).

Jonathan was saying that he wanted David to take his place as the next king of Israel!

Wow!

JESUS should be our closest friend. And we should be prepared to give everything we have to Him. We should put Him first in our lives.

Read verses 5-9

David was s_____ at everything (v5). So King Saul gave him a high rank in the a_____ (v5). David became so p_____ that the people sang s_____ (v6) about him! This made Saul a_____ and j_____.

Think!

Do you ever get jealous of people more popular or successful than you? Ask God to help you to fight your jealousy.

David, God's chosen king, was loved by some and hated by others. He reminds us of God's perfect King — Jesus. He causes very different reactions in different people (see John 7 v 42-44).

How do you react to Jesus and what He says in the Bible?

WEIRD WORDS

One in spirit
Really close friends

Covenant
Special agreement

Lyres
Harps

Refrain
Chorus

69

Spear in the ear!

**1 Samuel
18 v 10-16**

David is now an important officer in Saul's army. The Israelites love him and Jonathan thinks the world of him.

In fact, everyone thinks David is great.

Well, not quite everyone...

Saul is getting more and more jealous of David. Despite all his success, David's life is in danger. It wasn't a good idea to get on the wrong side of a king like Saul!

Read 1 Samuel 18 v 10-16

Are you ready for some quickfire questions? Have a go at these...

What did Saul throw at David?

a) a spear ☐

b) a deer ☐

c) a ginger beer ☐

Why was Saul afraid of David?

a) he was big and strong ☐

b) the Lord was with him ☐

c) he had a rottweiler ☐

So what did Saul do?

a) sent David with the army ☐

b) sent him to prison ☐

c) stamped his feet and cried ☐

In everything, David was...

a) useless ☐

b) annoying ☐

c) successful ☐

B_____ T_____
SACUBEE HET

L_____ W_____
DORL SAW

W_____ H_____
THIW MHI

But how can we be sure that God is with us? **1 Kings 11 v 38** gives us the answer:

If you do whatever I command you and walk in obedience to me and do what is right in my eyes by obeying my decrees and commands, as David my servant did, I will be with you.

Think & pray!

Are you a Christian? Do you live for God and try to serve Him in everything you do? There's great news: GOD IS WITH YOU! Spend time telling God how that makes you feel.

Why was David so unbelievably successful (v14)? Unscramble the anagrams to find out.

Blood and marriage

**1 Samuel
18 v 17-30**

*King Saul is
getting more
and more
jealous and
afraid of David
and his success.*

*But what will
Saul do about
it?*

WEIRD WORDS

Snare
Trap

Foreskins
Part of the skin on
the penis

Attendants
Servants

Allotted
Chosen

Elapsed
Passed

*Today's missing words can all be
found in the backwards word pool.*

selttab evol desaelp
thgif bareM wal-ni-nos
senitsilihP roop
divaD dellik
002 edausrep eid
deirram efiw lahciM
droL dairfa niks

Read 1 Samuel 18 v 17-19

Saul offered David his
daughter M_____ to be
his w_____. In return, Saul
asked David to f_____
in b_____ for him.
Saul hoped that David
would be k_____
by the Philistines. But
D_____ turned down
the offer!

Read verses 20-23

Saul's other daughter,
M_____, was in l_____
with David. This p_____
Saul and he again asked
David to become his
s_____ He also got
his servants to
p_____ David. But
David thought he was too
p_____ to marry her.

In Bible times, a groom gave the
bride's father a load of money to
make up for the loss of a daughter
and to show that he would look
after her. Imagine how much
you'd have to give to a king! David
couldn't afford it.

Read verses 24-30

Instead of money, Saul
asked David to kill 100
P_____ and
bring back part of their
s_____. Saul hoped that
David would d_____ in
the battle. But David and
his men killed _____
Philistines, so David
m_____ Michal.
Saul became more
a_____ of David.

David didn't even know that Saul
was out to kill him! *So how did he
survive so many battles?*

The L_____ was with
David (v28)

Pray!

Thank the Lord that He looks
after His people, even when
they are not aware of it! (Can
you think of examples that have
happened to you?)

71

**1 Samuel
19 v 1-7**

King Saul was hugely jealous of David, and afraid of him too.

Saul wanted his son Jonathan to help him murder David.

But Jonathan was proving to be a great friend to David...

Friend in need

Spot two ways in which Jonathan helped David.

Read 1 Samuel 19 v 1-5

1. Well-timed warning (v2)

"My f__th__r S__ __l
is l__ __k__ng f__r a
ch__nc__ to k__ll y__ __"

Jonathan warned David just in time! The Lord was with David, but he still had to do what he could to protect himself.

2. Brave words (v4)

J__n__th__n sp__k__
w__ll __f D__v__d

Jonathan could have chickened out of talking to his father. But he stood up for his friend David, even in tricky circumstances.

Read verses 6-7

Jonathan's chat with Saul did the trick! The king promised not to kill David. Tomorrow we'll see if Saul kept his promise...

Make a quick list of some of your friends. Think of ways you can be a better friend to them.

Friend	What you can do

What was the most important thing that Jonathan said (v5)?

Th__ L__rd w__n
a gr__ __t v__ct__ry
f__r __sr__ __l

Jonathan reminded Saul that the Lord was with David when he defeated Goliath. It was **God** who was in charge, and He was protecting David.

Pray!

Thank God that He is in charge of your life. And thank Him for the friends He has given you. Ask Him to help you be a better friend to them.

72

Window of opportunity

**1 Samuel
19 v 8-17**

Yesterday, King Saul promised Jonathan that he wouldn't kill David.

But it didn't take Saul long to change his mind...

Read 1 Samuel 19 v 8-10

Unjumble the anagrams to reveal what happened.

D_____ and his men
v i d a D

a_____ the
e d k a t c a t

Philistines until they

f_____ (v8). Later, S_____
d e l f   l u S a

tried to a_____ David,
t a k t a c

so David f_____ (v10).
e f d l

Read verses 11-17

Saul's men were out to
k_____ David. But David's
l i k l

wife M_____ persuaded
c h a l i M

him to escape, and she
let him down through a
w_____ (v12).
w o w d i n

She then pretended that
David was i_____ in bed
l i l

so he could e_____.
s e e c a p

David was in great danger and had to keep running for his life from Saul.

Do you think David got angry with God for letting this happen?

YES/NO _____

It's easy to find out because David wrote **Psalm 59** about it.

Read Psalm 59 v 16-17

Amazing. David praised God for protecting him and keeping him safe! He knew that God had helped him to escape from Saul three times! (1 Samuel 19 v 2, 10, 12)

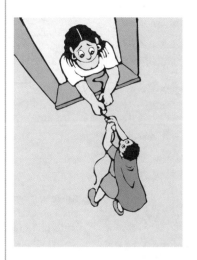

Think!

When life seems hard to you, do you blame God for the tough times?
Or do you praise and thank Him for looking after you, even in the hardest times?

WEIRD WORDS

Eluded
Escaped

Idol
Statue of a fake god

Prophet and loss

73

1 Samuel 19 v 18-24

David is on the run from Saul, who wants to kill him.

So far, God has kept David safe.

Now David has turned up at Samuel's house and he needs help. Fast!

God was going to protect David in an unusual way.

Read 1 Samuel 19 v 18-24

Saul found out where David was hiding and was determined to capture him and kill him.

How many groups of men did Saul send to capture David?

_____

How many of the groups of men joined in with the prophets instead of grabbing David?

_____

So who went in the end? (v23)

_____

There was nothing Saul could do because God was on David's side. Instead of grabbing David, Saul ended up praising God!

Who was looking after David?

_____

So who was in control?

_____

Think!

Do you ever feel as if you're in a corner, as David did? Are you afraid of being hassled for being a Christian? Are you afraid of the devil's attacks?

Wow!

Life can be scary for Christians sometimes. But God is on their side, helping them to serve Him!

Read what David said in **Psalm 32 v 7** *and fill in the gaps.*

You are my

_____; you will

_____ me from

_____.

Pray!

God looks after His people. Thank God for His love and protection.

WEIRD WORDS

Naioth
Part of the town of Ramah, where prophets lived

Prophesying
Praising God

Cistern
Pit where water is stored

Promising stuff

**1 Samuel
20 v 1-17**

*David is still
on the run,
and this time
he turns to his
friend Jonathan
for help. But
Jonathan is
also King Saul's
son...*

WEIRD WORDS

Grieved
Upset

**New Moon
feast**
Feast where they
praised God

Earnestly
Seriously

Inkling
Suspicion

**Favourably
disposed**
On your side

Covenant
Agreement

Read 1 Samuel 20 v 1-9

Today's key word is in verse 8.

COVENANT
which means
AGR__ __M__NT

Jonathan and David had made
an agreement to look after each
other (it's in 1 Samuel 18 v 3).
That's why David knew he could
turn to Jonathan. They'd made the
promise **before God** so God was
protecting David!

Wow!

Read Proverbs 29 v 25. God
promises to keep safe those who
trust in Him! So when Christians are
in trouble, they should turn to God
for help.

Read verse 4 again

Wh__t__v__r y__ __
w__nt m__ t__ d__, __'ll
d__ f__r y__ __.

Think!

Are you the kind of friend who puts
others first? Or do you just look
after yourself?

David asked Jonathan to warn him if
Saul still wanted to kill him.

Read verses 10-13

In Bible times, princes always killed
off their rivals. Yet Prince Jonathan
refused to kill his rival David, and he
kept his promise.

Action!

When you promise your friends
something, make sure you stick
to it!

Read verses 14-17

Sh__w m__ unfailing
k__ndn__ss (v14)

David promised to always show
kindness to Jonathan and all of
his family.

Pray!

Write down the name of
someone who's been a great
friend to you.

_____

Pray for them, thank God for their
friendship, and ask Him to help
you be a better friend to them.

Feast and furious

Things were getting really tricky for David.

Would he be safe from Saul, or would the king capture him?

WEIRD WORDS

Stone Ezel
Big rock or heap of stones

Abner
Commander of the army

Ceremonially unclean
Not clean enough to worship God

Perverse
Disobedient to God

Bore
Gave birth

Read 1 Samuel 20 v 18-23

Cross out the wrong choices.

Jonathan said: "Tomorrow is the NEW MOON/OLD SUN/ PINK STARS feast, and Saul will notice that you're not there. TOMORROW/THE DAY AFTER TOMORROW/ TUESDAY I'll come to where you're hiding and shoot three BARROWS/MARROWS /ARROWS. If I tell the boy that the arrows are this side of him, then you are IN DANGER/SAFE/STUPID. But if the arrows are FATTER/FILTHIER/FURTHER than the boy, then the Lord is sending you away."

Read verses 24-29

At the festival, Saul sat by the WALL/BALL/HALL, near Jonathan and Abner. But David's place was TAKEN/ EMPTY/ORANGE. Saul thought that David must be UNHEALTHY/UNDER THE TABLE/UNCLEAN. So when David didn't show up on the second day, Jonathan tried to make TROUBLE/EXCUSES/ EGG SANDWICHES for him.

Read verses 30-34

Saul was FURIOUS/FAIR with Jonathan and said that David must DANCE/DIET/DIE. He then hurled a SWORD/ SPEAR/SPOON at his son. Jonathan now knew that his father wanted to CATCH/ KILL/CONGRATULATE David.

Jonathan was expected to take his father's side and kill off any rivals like David. But Jonathan had made an agreement (covenant) with David.

He could have done what was easiest and best for himself and killed David. Instead, he kept his promise and stayed loyal to David.

Pray!

Ask God to guide you in your decisions. Ask Him to help you to put Him first — to serve and obey Him. Ask Him to help you not to just do what is easiest, most fun, or best for yourself.

Time to go...

*After Saul's
furious tantrum
at the feast,
Jonathan knew
that his father
wanted to kill
David!*

*It's time for
Jonathan to go
and warn his
friend...*

Jonathan and David agreed on a
secret code to let David know if he
was safe or not. (See yesterday's
Discover for a reminder.)

Read 1 Samuel 20 v 35-40

David knew that Saul was still
hunting him down and that he
wasn't safe near the palace. So he
was ready to run for his life.

> *Ever had a friend who had to
> move away?*

If so, you can imagine how David
and Jonathan felt.

Read verses 41-42

They knew this might be the last
time they'd see each other.

*What were Jonathan's parting
words? Go back one letter to find
out.*

$$\frac{}{H}\,\frac{}{P}\quad\frac{}{J}\,\frac{}{O}$$

$$\frac{}{Q}\,\frac{}{F}\,\frac{}{B}\,\frac{}{D}\,\frac{}{F}$$

Wait a minute! How can David
go in peace when he's in such
danger?!

Read verse 42 again

**We have promised to be
friends** $\frac{}{J}\,\frac{}{O}\quad\frac{}{U}\,\frac{}{I}\,\frac{}{F}$

$$\frac{}{O}\,\frac{}{B}\,\frac{}{N}\,\frac{}{F}\quad\frac{}{P}\,\frac{}{G}$$

$$\frac{}{U}\,\frac{}{I}\,\frac{}{F}\quad\frac{}{M}\,\frac{}{P}\,\frac{}{S}\,\frac{}{E}$$

God gave them peace in a
dangerous situation. And they
knew that they'd always be at
peace with each other, because
of the agreement (covenant) they
had made.

Think!

Is God at the centre of your
friendships? Think of two ways
in which your friendships could
please God more.

1. _____

_____

_____

2. _____

_____

_____

Now spend time talking to God,
asking Him to help you.

11 Praise in peril

Psalm 34 v 1-10

David's life was in constant danger.

Wherever he went, he knew people might recognise him and report back to Saul.

David wrote **Psalm 34** while he was on the run, pretending to be a madman!

Read Psalm 34 v 1-3

H	E	H	E	S	L	E	E	A
E	S	N	X	P	M	X	S	N
A	Y	S	T	D	U	A	I	S
R	C	N	O	A	F	L	A	W
D	R	M	L	L	M	T	R	E
S	A	V	E	D	B	D	P	R
G	L	O	R	I	F	Y	S	E
T	P	B	O	B	S	T	W	D
D	E	L	I	V	E	R	E	D

Find four words in the wordsearch that sum up how David feels towards God. The words (or similar ones) are in verses 1-3.

__X__ _L
       2

P__ _ _ _ _
  4

G__ _ _ _ _ _
     9   1

E__A__ _
        5

Even at this dangerous time David is bursting with praise for God!

Read verses 4-7

Find four more words that sum up what God had done for David (and what He does for all of His people).

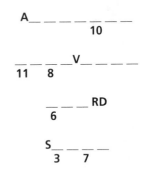

A_ _ _ _ _ _ _
              10

_ _ _ _V_ _ _ _
11   8

_ _ _ RD
6

S_ _ _ _
3   7

God had answered his prayers, rescued him from trouble, and kept him safe. No wonder David wanted to praise God!

Read verses 8-10

Sum up what David is saying by filling in the numbered letters in order (from 1-11).

— — — —

— — — — — — —

That means worship Him, trust Him, obey Him, love Him. David definitely did. DO YOU?

Pray!

Write a list of stuff to praise and thank God for. Then do it!

WEIRD WORDS

Extol
Praise

Afflicted
Suffering people

Rejoice
Be happy

Glorify
Give God praise and honour

Exalt
Lift up with praise

Delivered
Rescued

Radiant
Shining with joy

Takes refuge
Finds safety

Holy people
Believers

Daniel: God's in charge!

Daniel
7 v 1-7

Earlier in this issue we started reading all about Daniel.

He was taken away from Jerusalem and made to live in evil Babylon.

In Babylon, God used him to tell kings what their dreams meant.

All the time Daniel was in this foreign country he continued to serve God. He even refused to worship false gods and was thrown into a lion pit for it!

But God kept Daniel safe and the lions left him alone!

Read Daniel 7 v 1-3

God gave Daniel a vision. All the things in Daniel's dream mean something. For example, the "great sea" (v2) means the world, which was like a violent ocean, with nations fighting each other.

Read verses 4-7

Daniel dreamed of four terrifying beasts. *Go on, have a go at drawing them...*

> **Beast 1** (verse 4)

> **Beast 2** (verse 5)

> **Beast 3** (verse 6)

> **Beast 4** (verse 7)

Scary! The beasts stand for four different kingdoms (v17). (Kingdoms like Babylonia, Persia, Greece and the Roman Empire, who were all powerful at different times.) They represent humans ignoring God and fighting each other, trying to rule the world.

Wow!

It often seems as though evil people are in charge of the world and that God isn't. As we read the rest of Daniel, we'll see that it's God who is in control and will rule for ever!

Pray!

Pray for specific parts of the world where evil seems to be in charge. Ask God to do amazing things there.

WEIRD WORDS

Substance
What was in it

Authority to rule
God allowed it to be in charge

Throne zone

**Daniel
7 v 8-14**

We're in the middle of Daniel's terrifying dream.

Read Daniel 7 v 8

Daniel has already seen four powerful beasts. Next, a small one takes over. It may be small, but a horn means someone with **great power**. We'll find out who he is tomorrow.

Read verses 9-12

Daniel saw God on the throne — He's in control! He has always existed and always will! God rules for ever!

*Fill in the missing **H**s **O**s and **R**s to complete the description of God.*

His cl__t__es were w__ite as sn__w and His __ead and __air were w__ite (v9)

White is pure. God is pure and perfect. Everything He does is good and right.

His th__one was flaming with fi__e (v9)

In the Bible, fire is often a sign of judgment. God is in total control and will punish those who go against Him (v11).

Get ready for something else amazing! See if you recognise who is next to arrive...

Read verses 13-14

1. One like a S__n of man
That's the name Jesus called Himself (e.g. Matthew 9 v 6). Jesus was God's Son but He became a human being.

2. He was given auth__ __ity, gl__ry and sovereign p__we__
God made Jesus King, ruler of everything.

3. Pe__ple of all nati__ns w__ __s__ipped Him
One day everyone will bow down to Jesus!

4. God's kingd__m will neve__ be dest__ __yed
God's kingdom will rule for ever, after all human rulers and kingdoms are gone.

Pray!

Jesus wasn't just the tiny, weak baby we remember at Christmas. He is the powerful, conquering King. He will destroy all His enemies and everyone will worship Him. Spend time praising Jesus right now.

WEIRD WORDS

Ancient of Days
God, who has always existed

Slain
Killed

Glory
The honour and respect Jesus deserves

Sovereign power
Control of everything!

Dominion
Power, authority

Simply the beast

Daniel
7 v 15-28

*To remind
yourself of
Daniel's wild
dream, read
Daniel 7 v 1-14.*

*But what does
it all mean?
Daniel's about
to find out.*

WEIRD WORDS

**Holy people of
the Most High**
God's people,
Christians

Devoured
Ate

**Ancient of Days
/the Most High**
Both are names for
God

Subdue
Defeat, conquer

Oppress
Rule over cruelly

Sovereignty
Control over
everything

Read Daniel 7 v 15-18

The four terrifying beasts stand
for four powerful kingdoms that
would conquer many nations. But
the great news is that God's people
(Christians) will one day rule with
Him for ever (v18)!

Read verses 19-22

Daniel wanted to know about the
most terrifying beast with the iron
teeth. And also about the horn that
fought against God and His people.

Read verses 23-28

*Go forward one letter to complete
the explanation.*

___ ___ ___ '___
F N C R
___ ___ ___ ___ ___ ___ WILL
O D N O K D
___ ___ ___ ___ ___ (v25)
R T E E D Q

Kings would rule and kill many
people (v23). One king would even
speak against God and persecute
God's people (v25).

But...

___ ___ ___   ___ ___ ___ ___
S G D   J H M F

___ ___ ___ ___   ___ ___
V H K K   A D

___ ___ ___ ___ ___ ___ ___ ___ ___
C D R S Q N X D C

No-one is more powerful than God.
He will defeat all His enemies and
win victory for His people! (v26-27)

___ ___ ___   ___ ___ ___ ___
F N C   V H K K

___ ___ ___ ___   ___ ___ ___
Q T K D   E N Q

___ ___ ___ ___ (v27)
D U D Q

Christians will suffer for following
Jesus. But they can be certain
that God will defeat evil for ever!
And they will rule with God in His
kingdom for ever!

Pray!

Think of Christians who get a
hard time for following Jesus. Ask
God to help them through tough
times. Thank God that He will
defeat evil and will rule for ever!

81 Gruesome goat

God gave Daniel another vision. Ready to read about it?

WEIRD WORDS

Citadel
Fortress

Province
Area

Beautiful Land
Israel

Host of the heavens/starry host
Christians

Daily sacrifice
Gifts given to God

Sanctuary
God's temple

Rebellion
Sin against God

Desolation
Destruction

Reconsecrated
Fit to worship God there

Read Daniel 8 v 1-7

All of today's missing words are in the centre of the page.

Daniel saw a r____ with t____ horns (v3). It c_____ towards the west, north and s_____ (v4). No a_____ could stand up to it and it did as it p_____ (v4). Suddenly a g_____ with a horn between its e_____ came from the w_____ (v5). It attacked the ram and knocked it to the g_____, defeating it (v7).

Did you know that Daniel's dream matches up with real events in history? The ram represents the kings of Persia and the goat stands for Alexander the Great from Greece. Long after Daniel's dream, it all happened exactly as God had said. **He is the only God and everything He promises comes true!**

[centre word bank: animal charged earth eyes goat ground heavens horn mornings west 2300 two threw temple south sacrifice ram pleased animal]

Read verses 8-14

A small h_____ became very powerful (v9). It attacked the host (army) of the h_____ and t_____ some of them to the e_____ (v10). It took away the daily s_____ offered to the Lord and wrecked the temple (v11). It would be _____ evenings and m_____ before the t_____ was restored (v14).

This horn is probably Antiochus, an evil king who attacked God's people 400 years later. But it also warns **us** about our future. Christians will be attacked. And right now the devil wants to stop us worshipping God. But God helps us to stand firm. And He will defeat the devil!

Think & pray!

God's people (Christians) don't have temples and sacrifices any more. Jesus' death made it possible for us to go straight to God without needing priests, temples or sacrifices. Praise Jesus that nothing can take Him away! Then ask God to keep you strong and safe in your faith.

Sin is serious!

82

**Daniel
8 v 15-27**

*Remember
Daniel's vision
of the ram,
the goat and
the horn who
attacked God's
people?*

WEIRD WORDS

The Ulai
The canal in
Daniel's vision

Gabriel
Important angel

Fell prostrate
Bowed down

Son of man
Here it means
Daniel

Time of wrath
God punishing His
enemies

Intrigue
Lies and deception

**Prince of
princes**
God

Read Daniel 8 v 15-22

*What time does Gabriel say Daniel's
vision is all about? (v17)*

It's about the **end** of all these
terrible kings we read about
yesterday. And it's about the **end**
of the world, when Jesus will return
and evil will be beaten for ever!

Read verses 23-26

This is the evil king we read about
yesterday. He would kill thousands
of people and do many evil things,
even standing up to God Himself
(v25)! *But what would happen to
him? Take **every second letter** to
find out (starting with H).*

RHUEBWBIILSLHBR

EUDBEBSITSRHORYUEB

DBBIUSTHNROUTBBBYIH

SUHMRAUNBPBOIWSEHR

H_____

_____

_____

_____

This king persecuted God's people
so God destroyed Him! And one day
all evil will be punished. God will
win the victory!

Read verse 27

**How was Daniel after seeing his
vision?**

Really really happy ☐
Exhausted and ill for days ☐
As mad as a chicken ☐

**How did he feel about the
vision?**

Happy and relieved ☐
Not bothered ☐
Appalled and puzzled ☐

In his vision, Daniel saw how people
would sin against God again and
again. It made Daniel so sad he was
ill. But he soon got back to work,
serving God (v27).

Think!

When you see terrible things on the
news, or people around you sinning,
does it upset you?

It should, because people are
disobeying GOD, your King! But
we've still got to get on with life,
serving God until Jesus comes back
and sin is destroyed for ever.

Pray!

Ask God to help you take sin
more seriously, so that you hate
it. Ask Him to help you with sin
problems in your life.

83

Pray as you learn

Daniel
9 v 1-14

Today we get to peek at Daniel reading his Bible and praying.

Read Daniel 9 v 1-3

Jerusalem, Daniel's city, was ruled by the Babylonians.

Daniel read in the Bible book of Jeremiah that God would give the city back to the Israelites after 70 years of enemy rule. God would be merciful, but the Israelites were still sinning!

Think!

Daniel was really upset so he started praying straight away! Do things you read in the Bible cause you to act straight away? To say sorry to God or to thank Him for what you've learned? Why not try it, starting RIGHT NOW?

Read Daniel 9 v 4-10

Daniel pleaded with God to keep His promise.

Fill in the missing vowels (aeiou) to discover three great things about God.

1. God k__ __ps His c__v__n__nt (v4)

God always keeps His promises (covenants). He promised that Jerusalem would be given back to the Israelites, and it was! God also promises to always be with His people, and He is!

2. God always does wh__t is r__ght (v7)

We may not understand why bad things sometimes happen. But we can be sure that God is doing the best thing for us, and that His plans will work out.

3. God is m__rc__f__l and f__rg__v__ng (v9)

We disobey God again and again, yet He continues to forgive His people! And He gives us far more than we deserve!

Read verses 11-14

God was so brilliant to the Israelites. Daniel felt terrible about how they had treated God.

Pray!

Do you realise how brilliant God has been to you? Does it make you feel bad about how you've treated Him? Say sorry to God for wrong things you've done recently. Then thank Him that He always keeps His promises and is so forgiving.

WEIRD WORDS

Darius
The king who threw Daniel into the pit of lions

Desolation
Devastation, ruin

Petition
Asking God to do something

Sackcloth and ashes
A sign of sadness

Covenant
Agreement between God and His people

Righteous
Right and perfect

Merciful
Amazingly forgiving

Transgressed
Disobeyed

84

**Daniel
9 v 15-19**

Daniel is praying. He's asking God to keep His promise and give Jerusalem back to the Israelites.

Give God the glory

All of today's missing words can be found in the wordsearch.

J	R	L	B	T	N	A	M	E
S	E	P	M	S	Z	N	Y	G
Q	C	R	D	I	P	G	P	Y
S	C	A	U	N	X	E	E	P
I	D	Y	J	S	N	R	O	T
N	K	E	L	C	A	F	P	E
F	V	R	F	I	M	L	L	A
U	B	S	A	T	U	H	E	J
L	G	O	N	Y	C	R	E	M

Read Daniel 9 v 15-16

Lord, you brought your
p_____ out of
E_____ (v15). Turn your
a_____ away from
J_____ (v16).
Our s_____ have made
other nations look down on
your people (v16).

Daniel remembered how God brilliantly rescued the Israelites from Egypt (you can read about it in the Bible book of Exodus). So Daniel knew that God could rescue His people again.

Think!

Do you remember the good things God has done in your life? Do you even notice when He answers your prayers? *Write down some of the things God has done for you...*

_____

_____

_____

_____

Read verses 17-19

God, hear our
p_____ to rescue
Jerusalem (v17). We are
s_____ but you show
great m_____ (v18).
Please rescue Jerusalem
because this c_____ and
people are yours. They bear
your N_____ (v19).

Daniel wasn't just praying for himself and his people. He was most concerned that **God** got the respect and glory He deserved — that people worshipped God in His city and temple again.

Pray!

How different are Daniel's prayers to yours? Make sure you pray for things that please God and give God the glory.

WEIRD WORDS

Righteous
Right, perfect

Wrath
Punishment

Iniquities
Disobedience

Object of scorn
God's people were ridiculed by other nations

**Desolate
sanctuary**
Wrecked temple

Mercy
Undeserved forgiveness

Mind-boggling message

**Daniel
9 v 20-27**

Daniel has been asking God to rebuild Jerusalem and give it back to His people. Immediately God sent His answer.

Read Daniel 9 v 20-26

God's message to Daniel is mind-boggling! Let's try to work it out.

What number is mentioned most?

All these "sevens" mean seven weeks or years. But they're not precise periods of time. God is just telling Daniel what He will do in the future.

What would happen in the first period of time? (v25)

_____

_____

_____

_____

Wow! God would keep His promise to rebuild Jerusalem. He would forgive His people for turning away from Him and they would live His way again.

After Jerusalem was rebuilt, God's chosen King ("*Anointed One*") would come. That's **Jesus**. But He would be violently killed (v26). Then Jerusalem and God's temple would be destroyed again.

Read verse 27

Sacrifices to God would end because **Jesus** was the ultimate sacrifice. He died so that people can have their sins forgiven. They can now go straight to God for forgiveness. They don't need to offer sacrifices anymore!

I'm not sure exactly what the **abomination that causes desolation** (awful horror) in verse 27 is. But other Bible bits show that it's set up by God's enemy to turn God's people away from Him. But God has already ordered its end.

Pray!

Remember the most important thing — JESUS is at the centre of God's plans. His death makes it possible for anyone to turn back to God and have their sins forgiven. THANK God for sending Jesus to rescue His people so they can be with God again.

WEIRD WORDS

His holy hill
Jerusalem, city of God's people

Gabriel
An angel, God's messenger

Esteemed
God thought highly of Daniel

Decreed
Commanded

Transgression
Sin

Atone
Deal with the sin and forgive them

Anointed One
King Jesus

Sanctuary
God's temple

Covenant
Promise

Shining example

Guess what!
Daniel had
ANOTHER
amazing vision...

WEIRD WORDS

Cyrus
King who took
over Babylon when
Daniel was nearly
90

Mourned
Was very upset

Topaz
Shiny jewel

Multitude
Large crowd

Highly
esteemed
Well thought of by
God

Detained
Kept busy

Read Daniel 10 v 1-9

Complete the labels below that
describe Daniel's vision.

Dressed in _____ **(v5)**

Eyes like _____
_____ **(v6)**

Voice sounded like _____
_____**(v6)**

Belt of _____**(v5)**

Body like _____**(v6)**

Arms and legs shining like
_____ **(v6)**

Wow! Daniel was given a vision of
Jesus! He saw how awesome and
powerful and impressive Jesus is. No
wonder Daniel felt so weak!

Read verses 10-12

God heard Daniel's prayer and sent
a messenger to answer Him.

Find two ways that God describes
Daniel in verse 12.

1. You set your mind to gain
u_____

Daniel tried to understand more and
more about God. We know that he
read his Scriptures (Bible) regularly.

2. You h_____ yourself

Daniel knew how powerful God was
and how he must live with God in
control of his life.

We should follow Daniel's example.
If we learn more about God and let
Him have control of our lives, we'll
grow closer to God, understand
more what He says, and trust Him
better.

Read verses 13-14

It's not just humans who have wars.
There's a spiritual war going on
too. The devil and his demons (and
people who reject God) fight God,
His people and His angels. Jesus was
busy with all this, but He hadn't
forgotten Daniel's prayer!

Pray!

Thank God that He will defeat the
devil. Ask God to help you learn
more about Him and let Him be
in control of your life.

Lip service

Daniel 10 v 15 – 11 v 1

Daniel has just had a vision of God and of the spiritual war that's going on.

Daniel is feeling really weak after seeing those amazing things...

WEIRD WORDS

Anguish
Fear and worry

Book of Truth
The true things about the future that He's about to tell Daniel

Darius the Mede
King Darius who threw Daniel into the lion pit

Use the backwards word pool to fill in today's missing words.

aisreP　dehcuot　eceerG

ehtaerb　htgnerts　hturT

leahciM　leinaD　kooB

spil　sselhceeps

Read Daniel 10 v 15-19

The Lord came to
D_____. Daniel
was so weak, he was
s_____ (v15).
A man touched Daniel's
l_____ and he was able
to speak (v16). Daniel said
that his s_____ was
gone and he could hardly
b_____ (v17). So the
man t_____
Daniel again, giving him
strength (v18).

Think!

We sometimes feel weak and useless. But God can give us the strength to keep going, to keep serving Him. Do you need to ask God to give you strength today?

Read Daniel 10 v 20 – 11 v 1

Complete what the man said.

Soon I will return to
fight the prince of
P_____, then the
prince of G_____ will
come. No one supports
me against the enemy
except M_____. But
first I'll tell you what's
written in the B_____ of
T_____.

Lots of wars were being fought in Daniel's time. Soon the Greeks would defeat the Persians. It looked bad for God's people, the Israelites. But behind the scenes, God's angels (like Michael) were fighting for God's people.

Wow!

There are loads of wars and terrifying things still happening in the world today. Sometimes it seems as if God is just leaving the world alone. But God is there behind the scenes and He's in control of everything!

Pray!

Think of some of the rotten things going on in the world right now. Ask God to help people in those horrible situations. Pray that people will turn to Him even in these desperate circumstances.

North v south

**Daniel
11 v 2-13**

A mysterious man is telling Daniel what will happen in the future.

Which nations will be powerful?

WEIRD WORDS

Parcelled out towards the four winds of heaven
Divided up and ruled by different nations

Allies
Fighting on the same side

Realm
Where the other king rules

Muster
Gather

Read Daniel 11 v 2-4

Now cross out the false answers.

There will be four kings of PERSIL/PERSIA (v2). The fourth will stir up everyone against GREECE/GREASY FOOD (v2). Then a mighty KING/QUEEN/JOKER will rule with great power (v3). That would be Alexander the Great of Greece, who defeated Persia and many other nations. But his empire would be BEST/BROKEN UP (v4).

Read verses 5-10

The king of the South (Egypt) will become STRONG/AVERAGE/WEAK (v5), but one of his commanders would take over. The king of Egypt's DOG/DAUGHTER (v6) would make an alliance with the king of the North (Syria).

But someone from her SCHOOL/FAMILY will take her place (v7). He will defeat the King of SPAIN/SYRIA/SYRUP and take their false BEARDS/GODS back to Egypt (v8). Years later, Syria will gather a huge ARMADILLO/ARMY to attack Egypt (v10).

Read verses 11-13

Egypt will DEFEAT/TEASE Syria's huge army (v11) and the king of Egypt will FORGIVE/SLAUGHTER thousands of people (v12). But the king of Syria will gather an even SMALLER/LARGER/FATTER army (v13).

God told Daniel great details of what would happen in the future (we'll read more tomorrow). All of these things came true hundreds of years later! In ancient history books you can read how Alexander the Great defeated the Persians. And how Egypt and Syria fought many fierce battles.

Wow!

God knew all these things would happen because He was in control. Even though these mighty kings seemed to be in charge, it was all part of God's perfect plans.

Pray!

Praise God that He's in control and is more powerful than any king or president or army.

Making a stand

Daniel
11 v 14-35

Daniel is still being told about the future. *Cross out the wrong words.*

Read Daniel 11 v 14-20

Look at what this shows us about rulers...

- They capture/capsize each other's cities (v15)

- They do what pleases themselves/God (v16)

- They marry off their family to overcrowd/overthrow other kingdoms (v17)

- They are insolent/innocent (v18)

- They tax people so they can live in Luxembourg/luxury (v20)

All of these people please themselves. None serve God.

WEIRD WORDS

Beautiful land
Israel

Insolence
Disrespect

Contemptible
Deserving to be hated

Intrigue
Crafty plans

Provinces
Large areas of land

Holy covenant
God and His promises

Forsake
Turn away from

Desecrate
Ruin

Violated the covenant
Turned against God

Read verses 21-28

Look at how one leader becomes strong...

- He uses intrigue/insects to invade another kingdom (v21)

- He acts deceitfully/deliciously (v23)

- He salutes/steals from other kingdoms (v24)

- He sells ties/tells lies

But God defeats him!

Read Daniel 11 v 28-35

Daniel learned about a king who was against God's covenant with Israel and who supported people who turned against God.

But God's people stood up to him and refused to turn away from God (v32)! They continued teaching people about God even though many of them were captured or murdered (v33)!

Check out **John 15 v 18-19**. You could write it out on spare paper.

Wow!

Our world today is just the same. If we stand up for God, and tell people about Jesus, we will suffer. But it's a privilege to serve God. Jesus went through far more pain and suffering for us, so that one day we can live with Him in perfect peace for ever!

Pray!

Ask God to help you tell people about Jesus and not give up, no matter how hard it seems.

Rise and fall

**Daniel
11 v 36-45**

Daniel is being told about a future king who would turn against God and His people.

Read Daniel 11 v 36-39

What was this king like?
Tick two answers.

He served God ☐

He pleased himself ☐

He put others first ☐

He thought he was better than God ☐

Evil will be defeated! The devil won't win! When Jesus died and rose back to life, He defeated sin and the devil. The victory will be completed when Jesus returns! How brilliant is that?!

WEIRD WORDS

Exalt and magnify
Lift himself up to be worshipped

Time of wrath
When God will punish sinners

Acknowledge
Support him as king

Cavalry
Army on horses

Edom, Moab and Ammon
Israel's enemies

Lybians and Cushites in submission
Other countries serving him

Annihilate
Totally wipe out

Holy mountain
Jerusalem

He was a very foolish, evil man. But many people put themselves first and refuse to live God's way. Anyone who rejects God will end up defeated like this king. **Everyone** who rejects God will one day be punished.

Read verses 40-45

These verses say how the evil king would be defeated. But they're also about the very end of time. The **devil** is like this king. At times it seems as though he's winning. There is so much sin in the world and so many people live for themselves instead of God. It can all seem depressing.

But read verse 45 again

In the box, sum up the king's reign and what happened to him.

Pray!

Spend time thanking and praising God for defeating the devil. If you're a Christian, you're on the winning team!

Tomorrow we'll find out what will happen to God's people...

Daniel
12 v 1-4

*Want to know
what will happen
at the end of the
world?*

Then listen up...

Shining examples

Read Daniel 12 v 1

*Complete the great description by
filling in the missing vowels.*

1. Rescue!

**When Jesus returns at the
end of the world, it will be
terrifying. But ev__ry__n__
wh__s__ n__me is wr__tt__n
in the b__ __k will be
d__l__v__r__d.**

That means all God's people
(Christians) will be rescued! Life
before then may be really tough but
God will gather His people to live
with Him for ever in a perfect place.

Read verse 2

2. The living dead!

**Many who are d__ __d
(*sleeping in dust*) will
w__ke up. Some to
__v__rl__st__ng l__f__ and
others to everlasting
sh__me.**

Dead people will be brought back
to life! People who have lived God's
way will live with Him for ever.
Those who have lived their own way
won't.

Think!

Which group of people do you
belong to? If you're not sure, please
talk to an older Christian about it.

Read verses 3-4

3. Shining examples!

**The w__s__ will sh__n__
like the br__ghtn__ss of the
h__ __v__ns. Those who lead
many to r__ght__ __ __sn__ss
will sh__n__ like st__rs**

The wise means everyone who has
lived God's way. God will reward
them with eternal life. Especially
those who lead others to be rescued
by Jesus. The future for God's
people will be amazing!

Pick the prayer that fits you best...

Pray! 1

If you've not yet become a
Christian, talk to God about it.
Tell Him how you feel. Ask Him to
show you what to do.
For the factsheet *How to become
a Christian* email us at:
discover@thegoodbook.co.uk

OR

Pray! 2

If you are a Christian, you've
got so much to look forward to!
Spend time thanking God. Ask
Him to help you lead your friends
to Jesus.

WEIRD WORDS

Michael
The angel who
protects God's
people

Delivered
Rescued

Multitudes
Loads of people

**Everlasting
contempt**
They will suffer
God's punishment
for ever

Righteousness
Being forgiven by
God

That's all folks!

**Daniel
12 v 5-13**

*Congratulations!
You've reached
the end of
Daniel's book.*

*Are you as
confused as
Daniel is?*

WEIRD WORDS

Holy people
God's people

**Purified, made
spotless and
refined**
Forgiven, made
acceptable to God

Daily sacrifice
Gifts offered to
God every day

Abolished
Cancelled

**Allotted
inheritance**
Eternal life

God has revealed to Daniel loads
of things that would happen in the
future and at the end of time. But
when will these things happen? And
what exactly will happen?

Read Daniel 12 v 5-12

> **How long before these things
> happen? (v6)**

Daniel is given several
answers (v7, 11 and 12). But we
shouldn't worry too much about
these numbers. What Daniel learned
is that **God is in control**. It's God
who decides when things happen,
and only God knows when
Jesus will come at the
end of the world.

> **What will be the
> outcome? (v8)**

Daniel isn't given an
answer! The truth is, there are
some things we just can't
understand. Maybe we'll understand
them when we go to live with God.
But we can trust that **God is in
control**, and His perfect plans
will work out!

*But Daniel isn't left in the dark. He
is told two great things. Fill in the
missing letters to reveal what Daniel
is told.*

Read verse 13

1.   Go your __ay to the
     __nd. Be __aithful __o
     the __nd.

Daniel is told to **keep going!**

That's great advice for Christians.
We don't know when Jesus will
return. And we'll suffer for telling
people about Him. But we know
that He **will** return. So we've got
to stick at it, living God's way and
telling people about Jesus.

2. At the end of __ime you
    will __ise to __eceive
    your __nheritance.

When Jesus returns, all Christians
will be raised back to life and
will receive God's amazing gift:
everlasting life in heaven. How cool
is that?

Pray!

You're on your own today. Read
those last two things and talk to
God about whatever is on your
mind. (Be honest!)

DISCOVER
COLLECTION

ISSUE 12

DISCOVER ISSUE 12

Enter the royal court of King David in 1 and 2 Samuel. Learn how to build your life on God from Nehemiah. And watch as Jesus pays the ultimate price for his friends in Luke's Gospel.

DISCOVER

BIBLE NOTES FOR YOUNG PEOPLE

THREE MONTHS OF EXPLORING GOD'S WORD:
* **1 & 2 Samuel:** King David rules!
* **Nehemiah:** Life building
* **Luke:** The big finale

ISSUE 12

COLLECT 12 THE SET

COLLECT ALL 12 ISSUES TO COMPLETE THE DISCOVER COLLECTION

Don't forget to order the next issue of Discover. Or even better, grab a one-year subscription to make sure the next Discover lands in your hands as soon as you need it. Packed full of puzzles, prayers and pondering points.